pithy

adjective, pith·i·er,
pith·i·est.

"the important or essential part;
essence; core; heart"
Random House Unabridged Dictionary,
© Random House, Inc. 2006.

"Concise and full of meaning."
Wiktionary at www.en.wiktionary.org

CONTENTS

HOW THIS BOOK WORKS

The book isn't divided into chapters so much as notes. Each deals with a specific aspect of business we have found particularly pertinent on our own journey through the business corridors. To make life a little easier, we've grouped the notes into categories.

... 8   **FOREWORD**

... 11 **THINKING**

Before you even get to the planning stage of your business projects, there are a few things to keep in mind - particularly if you like to think of yourself as a strategic thinker with an eye on what's ahead rather than what is just under your nose in the here and now.

...	13	If You Can't Say it in a Sentence, You Just Don't Get it
...	17	Failing to Plan is Planning to Fail
...	20	Strategic Planning: Not Fast Forwarding the Past
...	23	Don't Boil the Ocean
...	27	The Marvel of the Matrix
...	33	Hands-On Ansoff
...	38	Ockham's Razor
...	41	Palimpsest: Making New From Old
...	46	See Things as If for the First Time
...	49	The DNA Test – Do Not Assume
...	53	Know What You Don't Know (and Know what you Know)
...	58	Pithy Pearls

... 59 DOING

Happy you've thought everything through? Preparation and planning done? Now you can dive in and focus on the active "doing" part.

... 60	Know Your Customer
... 66	Carpe Diem – Don't Ask Permission – Seek Forgiveness
... 72	Authority is Never Given. It is Taken
... 77	Don't Confuse Activity with Results
... 81	Don't Confuse Quality with Perfection
... 86	Brake Into the Corner, Accelerate Out
... 90	Don't Take the Monkey on Your Back
... 93	Pithy Pearls

... 95 LEADING

Being a good manager is not the same as being a good leader. In this section, we offer a few suggestions you should consider in your drive towards the top position.

... 96	Wherever My People Go I must Follow (For I am Their Leader)
... 100	Don't Dither. Decide.
... 105	Skip-Level Meetings
... 109	Job on the (Time)line

... 114	Don't Bring Me Problems. Bring me Solutions
... 117	Don't Tell Me What You Can't Do. Tell Me What You Can Do
... 122	Don't Mind Prima Donnas (As Long As They Can Sing)
... 126	The Two E-Mail Rule
... 130	Pithy Pearls

... 131 REWARDING

Human beings generally only do the stuff that they know will result in recognition or reward. Few of us are evolved enough to perform for the heady reward of self-realisation. If you want results from your team, get the ground rules of reward and measurement in place.

... 132	Contracts and Performance are by Mutual consent
... 138	Measure Right, Reward Right
... 142	Don't Praise a Fish for Swimming
... 146	Don't Just Praise Ideas. Praise Delivery

... **150**   Employees Want to Have Fun

... **155**   Pithy Pearls

... **157**   # SURVIVING
(The Stuff You Don't Get in Business Books)

We'd love to tell you that if you follow the rules of business etiquette and keep your nose pointed up towards the top of the ladder, you'd be fine. Truth is, you won't be. Survival in business means knowing some of the stuff they don't teach you at business school.

... **158**   Foregone Collusion

... **162**   You've Only Sold an Idea when it becomes Someone Else's Idea

... **165**   Corporate Jujitsu – Better to Deflect than Confront

... **169**   How Machiavellian!

... **172**   Machiavellian Prince-iple: Fake it 'til You Make It

... **174**   Machiavellian Prince-iple: Only the Paranoid Survive

... **176**   Don't Believe in Your Own Publicity

... **179**   Keeping Good Company

... **184**   Your Bit of the Planet

... **187**   Pithy Pearls

... **188**   PITHY POP-BIZ
A few last pithy phrases for you to chew on

... **189**   WILLEM The CV Stuff
Known in the business world as curriculum vitae. Don't worry, this is the abbreviated (pithy) version.

... **190**   WENDY The CV Stuff
Ditto. The abbreviated CV bit

... **192**   A Word or 2 of Thanks

... **194**   Bibliography

Foreword

This book is for managers.
And aspiring managers.
And staff members who want to understand their managers.

George Bernard Shaw famously said, "Gentlemen, you'll have to excuse me while I make a long speech as I didn't have time to prepare a short one."

After 18 years running my own business working for the corporate market of South Africa and a further 11 years working inside the corridors of a major financial services corporation, I've had my fill of men and women who mistake countless meetings for output and lengthy ramblings for business wisdom.

In the world of business, less is definitely more.
In this fast-moving world of advanced technology, digital communication, virtual teams and swift innovation, you have to get to the point quickly.
But the art of being pithy is beyond the issue of time.
What do you do when you can't pinpoint the answer

to a question? You talk around it, right? You describe it. It's not an issue of communication. It's an issue of understanding.

I am a communicator. I talk in visual images and like to tell stories. Willem is a hard-core business talker. He's a "less is more" kind of fellow. We meet in the middle, most of the time, and the result is a colourful and cluttered business Zen. We're both voracious readers but when it comes to business, we don't have time or inclination to wade through epistles that would better serve as doorstops than meaningful sources of business wisdom.

Taking the Pith Out of Business is not a new and innovative perspective on some five-sided business model that will make you rich beyond your dreams. It's not a "how-to" book of sales, answering the telephone or even managing teams. It is a collection of practical wisdom that is all about "been-there-done-that", not an academic tome. We'd like to think it offers some useful crib notes on how to be an excellent manager.

Willem has been running companies since he was twelve. Well, almost. He's mentored more individuals than I've had hot breakfasts. Over the years, I've noticed how he likes to distil ... well everything, actually ... down to a tidy little phrase. He is pithiness personified.

"That's good," I said one day when Willem rolled one of his newest and shortest truisms off his tongue. "That's a useful perspective on planning."
"Why don't you write it down?" he replied modestly. "Maybe we can come up with some more."

So I did.
And we did.
And here they are.

Wendy Coetzee

This book is a collection of management principles and guidelines that I have found particularly useful during my 35 years in corporate corridors. I am known for having a tidy desk devoid of paper. And my colleagues have become used to my disposition towards keeping things short and to the point. Wendy has added a few of her own. Naturally I had to edit them down. But that's what I do best.

Why say more when less is better?

Willem Coetzee

THINKING

"I like to tell people that all of our products and business will go through three phases. There's vision, patience, and execution."

Steve Ballmer
Chief Executive Officer, Microsoft Corporation

THINKING

A Story of Survival

Failed in business twice (1831 and 1834);

ran for US legislature in 1832 ... and lost;

Watched his sweetheart die in 1835;

Suffered a nervous breakdown in 1836;

Lost a bid for a seat in politics in 1838;

Was defeated in bids for US Congress three times:

(1843, 1846 and 1848);

Defeated for US Senate in 1855 and again in 1858;

Lost bid to become US Vice President in 1856.

But ...

this man became the 16th president of the United States in 1860.

His name was Abraham Lincoln.

He was a survivor.

THINKING

If you can't say it in a sentence ...
You just don't get it!

"Bullshit...", they say, "... baffles Brains". Long-winded explanations are a clear indication that the person doing the talking doesn't understand the true essence of what he or she is trying to sell. At your next dinner party, ask one of the guests a usual small-talk question "What do you do for a living?" and then ask them to *explain* that. Inevitably you'll hear qualifying explanations with much hand waving and bubble-descriptions rather than the essence of what they are doing. Pithiness is rarely the first call.

This is not a chapter on the importance of good communication skills. It's more pertinent than that. If you cannot simply and briefly explain your company (or presentation/ concept/great new idea/role/job description) then *you still don't really get* it.

What business is the drill manufacturing division of Black & Decker in? Selling drills, right? Wrong. Black & Decker Drills are in the business of selling holes. Simple, no-fuss, self-created holes. The drill is just the piece of equipment that gets you there.

Sanlam is a financial services company that sells mainly risk products and long-term investment products. But that's not the essence of their business. The true essence is they look after a person's financial future, hence their slogan "thinking ahead". Metropolitan, the company where Willem and I both worked for over a decade, would tell you they are about "financial wealth and health".

And then in the same industry, different sector: Chartis, the insurance-company-previously-known-as-AIG, is in the business of selling short-term insurance. Right? Wrong. Bob Gordon, chairman of the South African arm of the international company, describes the essence of their offering as "We sell peace of mind."

Cunard, owners of the Queen Mary cruise liner, originally developed a business model based on transporting passengers across water. But their business was more than passenger transport. Their real insight came when they realised "We're in the floating hotel business".

Now **that** you can sell.

And it fundamentally changed the way they did business. If Cunard were in the business of transporting passengers, their focus would fall on how to transport as many people as cheaply and efficiently as possible.

Queen Mary as she leaves Cape Town, February 2011.

However, if you are in the floating hotel business, you are in the hospitality and leisure industry. And that's a whole different can of sardines.

This is more than getting the words in order. It's about capturing the essence of who you are and what makes you different. Distilling this essential understanding of what your job is, what your product is about or what your company does into a single, simple statement will fundamentally change how you go about your business.

TAKE-OUT: Identify the essence of your job, your business, your project or even your Great New Idea and then translate it into an easy-to-understand sentence. If you have to ramble through an explanation, ask yourself if you really understand it? You know what you sell, but do you know what business you are in? Check it and double-check it. Only then can you roll out the planning sessions and get the troops into the frontline of the *right kind of* activity.

▶▶ PITHY PLAN

- ▶▶ Assemble a workshop session of key people who know the business and who represent most parts of the business.
- ▶▶ Start with the long-winded explanation. Capture words, phrases and thoughts that best describe your business (or project).
- ▶▶ Group the thoughts. Distil them down to essence. Distilling is not the same as summarising. Check the conclusions from all angles and from all people's point of view, inside the company and outside.
- ▶▶ When you have your single, simple sentence - test it. Do your customers and colleagues understand it the way you intend it to be understood? And is this really the business you are in?

THINKING

Failing to Plan
is Planning to Fail!

We know. It happened to us in Toledo, Spain.

We were on a trip with the top-performing - and hence award-winning - members of Metropolitan's Group Technology and Strategy division. Our bus was parked - **not** within walking distance - at the entrance to the magical walled city of Toledo. It was a fine spring day and the sky was blue. At least, it was when we first fell out of the bus. By noon, clouds had moved in and the heavens opened. What do you do when you have less than eight hours, on a one-off visit, to explore a far-away kingdom of history? You brave the rain and get wet. And cold.

Nobody had brought raincoats.

Nobody, that is, except for our workshop facilitator and his wife. Christo is a wisecracking and understated man, not known for verbosity. But whatever words he does use, count. He and his wife trotted past the two soggily miserable but doggedly determined Coetzees, happily wrapped in dense waterproof raincoats that provided head to toe warmth and dryness. As they drew ahead of us, Christo moved his mouth out of the protective cocoon of his hood.

"Failure to Plan," he said evenly, "Is Planning to Fail."

And kept on walking.

It was one of Those Moments. But reflecting back, those words are one of the fundamental philosophies of the corporate world. Things in life (whether you are inside the air-conditioned sanctuary of an office or in rural Spain) often don't go according to plan. As a manager, there is no such thing as over-preparation.

There are a thousand other ways of putting it. *Expect the unexpected. Plan for all consequences.* Be thorough in your preparation. We even have another version of it elsewhere in this book. *Do Not Assume.* But, at the end of the day, it comes down to what our friend Christo reminded us. And Benjamin

Franklin, of course, who was the first guy to come up with the quote!

TAKE-OUT: It's hard to improve on what George and Christo expressed so perfectly... if painfully. Failure to plan really is planning to fail.

▶▶ PITHY PLAN

- ▶▶ Call a planning session. Use sticky notes to capture everything.
- ▶▶ Rule of thumb, there are six basic questions to be answered when you do your planning.
    - ▶ Focus on What you have to do;
    - ▶ How this needs to happen;
    - ▶ Who is involved and responsible;
    - ▶ Understand the Why of what you are doing;
    - ▶ Then there is the When things have to happen. Timelines are imperative. No good promising the earth if delivery is open-ended;
    - ▶ Finally determine How Much you can spend.

THINKING

Strategic Planning NOT *fast forwarding* the Past

Strategic planning demands that you analyse the past. And projecting into the future is essential. But you can't base your strategic plans on the belief that "it worked last year".

Nothing is sacred in the marketplace anymore. In days gone by, food was sold by the grocery stores, telephones by the telephone company and postal services by the post office. You got clothes from the fashion shop and withdrew money from the teller in the bank. Life was that simple. Not anymore. Nowadays, the trend is convergence selling. You can pick up a funeral policy alongside a pair of new shoes and draw cash while paying for the bread and milk. It's a veritable cauldron of new opportunities. Great for the innovators. Tough on the Old School.

And then there is the full-blown blast impact of technology on our lives and our planning. The world is literally turning faster. Technology is pushing us into new paradigms more quickly than most of us can predict. Our grandfathers would have had a hard time mapping out their long-term 20-point plan if they had lived in this speedy century. And yet still some of us base our strategic planning on what worked last year. No Can Do.

American Futurist and inventor Ray Kurzweil talks of the exponential reality of technological change. He reckons 100 years of progress from our history books translates into the 21st century equivalent of 20 000 years. And that's just at today's rate. He predicts that, very soon, we'll have to get our heads around an "exponential growth in the rate of exponential growth". But let's park that brain-stretch for the moment.

It's time to know that you don't know everything. And you definitely can't rely on the past to predict the future. Think lateral. Think broad. Know that the impossible regularly becomes probable.

TAKE-OUT: Don't plan the future based entirely on the past. This worked two generations ago. Not today. Whether you are talking about business indicators, the market place, the economic environment or how your clients behaved, none of these aspects necessarily have the same qualities or criteria as when you did your planning last time round. Don't discard the lessons of the past but make sure that you think broadly when you do your planning. The future ain't what it used to be!

▶▶ PITHY PLAN

- ▶▶ Start with what you know and what you expect. Research, analyse, project.
- ▶▶ Spot the trends. Don't use traditional sources of information. Refer to consumer trends, climate trends, economic predictions, fashion, business success stories.
- ▶▶ Now think out of the box. Blue sky your ideas. Give yourself permission, preferably with the input of some clever people around the table, to play the "what if" game.
- ▶▶ You don't know what the future is. 15 years ago, neither the cell phone phenomenon nor the webbed world would have received serious attention at a planning session.

THINKING

Don't Boil the Ocean

When dealing with a new concept or idea, the human mind generally goes through three distinct phases. The first is when you acquire a Simplistic Understanding of something. Take a big topic, like the study of quantum physics. Somebody really smart might give you a 30 second "sound bite" of what it is. You'll probably be told that quantum physics is all about energy. Your smart friend will briefly explain how this energy behaves. He might tell you that in "simple terms" quantum physics is based on the theory that energy exists in individual units just like matter does and not, as once thought, as a constant electromagnetic field. It is quantifiable. Hence the term.

Fine. Well, fine-ish. Your brain identifies with the words and on some level it makes sense. You "understand".

So you enter the second phase. You research. You read. You reference your few new facts. You read up about Max Planck, the physicist who first declared energy to be measureable in quanta. He kick-started a new way of looking at the world and won the Nobel Prize

> " Where most of us end up there is no knowing, but the hell-bent get where they are going."
>
> James Thurber

for his trouble. There's Albert Einstein (of course) who took the subject to a whole new level. Your research will lead you to Schrodinger's Cat (nothing to do with animal care) and the theory of multiple worlds. You might even get lost in one of them yourself.

What you have done is settle into the second phase of "complex understanding". You have masses and masses of data and information but your head is churning with a complete lack of clarity. In fact, ironically, the more you learn, the less you know.
So what happens next? If you persist with this journey, you'll eventually land up in a moment (that moment might be a day or week long) when your brain steps free of all the noise and you achieve a *profound* simple understanding.

The trouble is, most of us get stuck in the middle bit. We literally attempt to boil the ocean. I'm talking business now where the search and acquisition of knowledge has to lead to something concrete ... like a decision. We look at this vast amount of information and try to get an understanding of every single aspect. We become a walking oracle on the subject because we have so much knowledge shoehorned into our heads. We are prepared to bore dinner party guests and work colleagues alike with all this impressive stuff. But we remain there, trapped under the weight of knowledge and information.

The thing is, you need to make a decision, as best you can, with the knowledge you have. This requires a huge effort and demands questions like "so what does this mean in real terms", "this is what we *do* with this knowledge" and "here's how it really matters". Now make a decision based on that. You'll find with time that you either prove or disprove your theory and early standpoint. Either way, you'll have achieved progress.

TAKE-OUT: Learn to recognise the differences in these three levels of understanding. Its foolhardy to jump in with action if you're making decisions based on a first level understanding but beware the allure of endless data

accumulation and research that goes with phase two. Boiling the ocean is busy work but not smart. Sometimes boiling just a section of the ocean is enough to draw early conclusions.

▶▶ PITHY PLAN

- ▶▶ Gather facts and early data.
- ▶▶ Generate a working (intelligent, fact-based) hypothesis early in the process.
- ▶▶ Treat this as a possible road map. Call it a stake in the ground if you will.
- ▶▶ Now focus on this and work towards proving or disproving it. You'll get real results and clarity as a result.

P.S. (Just to set the record straight, we've experienced this three step process all the way through to the "aha" understanding of phase three. But not in quantum physics. There, Willem's paddling happily in the quagmire of phase two while I have barely made it out of the starting blocks of phase one.

Just so you know.)

THINKING

The Marvel of the Matrix

Willem is an essence man. What takes me 45 pages to explain, he can chisel down to a sassy and succinct one-pager. I once wrote a philosophical novel. The draft format was 760 pages. He told me he could nail the essence of the book's lessons into four good paragraphs. He probably could. It would have wrecked the story but that's beside the point.

Where we agree is in business. You have to distil business down to the simplest possible format and, in our opinion, the format that works best of all is the simple foursquare matrix. It provides you with a one-page visual presentation of the crucial components - and the possible variables - of a situation.

Let's say you are trying to figure out different scenarios for either a macro-strategy or for the planning process of a specific product. The first thing you do is identify the extremes. We're heading for a foursquare matrix, right? So you need a vertical line and a horizontal ... each with their own opposite or extremes. I'm going to draw on one example that we used recently.

We worked with a large Zimbabwean bank that wants to increase its e-commerce activities. First step was to agree on the two main components of our scenario planning with the main decision-makers of this bank. After much vigorous to-ing and fro-ing, these two main components came out as "business processes" and information or "data". In their digital world, everything could more or less fit under one of those two headings.

Now we needed two descriptions at opposite ends of the scale for each line to create the matrix. We made processes our vertical line on the matrix and decided on points of "External Access" (access by clients to the bank's computer systems) as being one extreme and processes that involved "Internal Access" (access by the bank's employees to the bank's computer systems) as the other. The horizontal line was for data, which we identified as being data necessary for "Simple Transactions" and, at the other end of the scale, data that carried some sort of "Value-Add" quality.

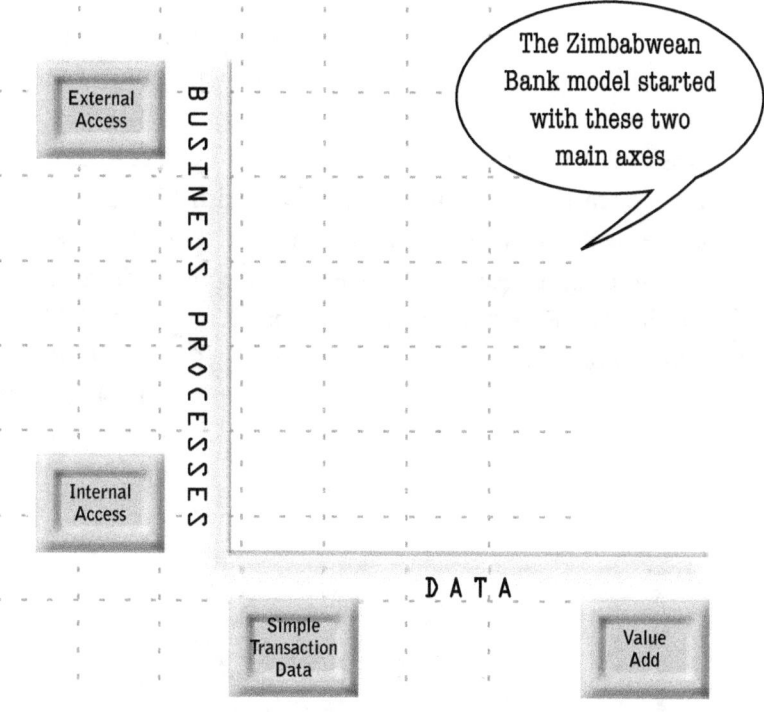

The most important rule of creating a working matrix is to make sure you get the variables (or critical factors) right. Get that wrong and you'll land up painstakingly creating a marvellous plan to bring about the wrong objectives. In the Zimbabwean bank workshop, that initial discussion took a whole day alone. But when we reached consensus, it was clear that at its simplest level, the components identified would cover everything we needed to embrace in a meaningful strategy.

Next step with a matrix is to join the dots. Or in this case, fill in the squares. What do you get where "Internal Processes" meets "Simple Transaction data"? We filled those in. And then we looked at what do you get when simple transaction data is paired up with "External processes"? We went through a similar conversation overlapping "internal Processes" with "Value Add" data and lastly, "External Processes" with "Value Add" data.

This is what we ended up with:

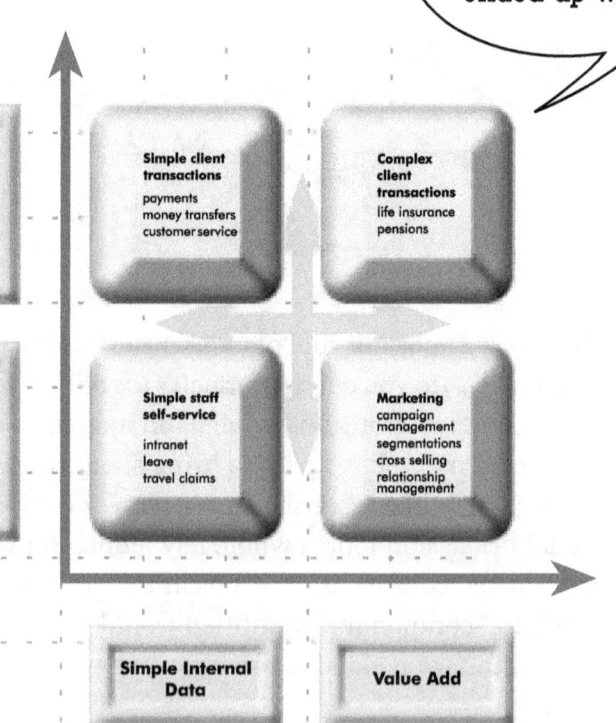

Neat, huh? You'd be amazed how useful this little model comes in, no matter what the subject. In the next chapter, we share the classic Ansoff marketing matrix where the focus falls on the interesting and ticklish relationship between market share and products.

The secret really lies in identifying the two humdinger components that are most important to the discussion. Not any old variables will do!

After you've pegged down the different options, it's a question of deciding which road you want to take. Perhaps you want to focus on one or two of the boxes in the matrix. Or perhaps your strategy demands that you embrace all four.

Besides helping to crystalise the "what" of your plan or strategy, this visual representation of your business model also forms useful "intel" when deciding what resources and personality types or skills sets to put where.

TAKE-OUT: Distil the main axis of your four-square matrix with enormous care. Garbage in your model merely proves garbage. Once you've got the picture-form of your plan in hand, you're better equipped to make decisions

relating to time, energy and resources ... and also differentiate how you present yourself to your client and suppliers.

▶▶ PITHY PLAN

- ▶▶ Be crystal clear about what you want to achieve or prove.
- ▶▶ Identify the key variables that would best represent the situation.
- ▶▶ Determine the extreme values that each of these two variables can take.
- ▶▶ Chalk them up and then populate the specifics within each of the four quadrants.
- ▶▶ Decide: do you go for all four quadrants or does it make sense to focus on one or two?

THINKING

Hands-On Ansoff

There is nothing new about the Ansoff Matrix but considering the fact that we staunchly stand by the merits of using matrix models in your business, we really need to share this one with you. It's the kind of thinking that is so common sense you might raise an eyebrow. However, as Voltaire sadly observed, "common sense is not that common". And if you miss this important strategic thinking tool, you could land your company in Deep Doggy Doo.

Harry Igor Ansoff left his native Russia (specifically the dramatic sounding Vladivostok) for the United States of America when he was just shy of his 20th birthday. His place in history began in 1957 when this Doctor of Applied Mathematics published an article in the Harvard Business Review entitled "Strategies for Diversification". And so the world was introduced to his "Product-Market-Growth" matrix, a marketing tool that went way beyond its original "marketing" intention to become one of the most fundamental of all strategic tools.

The pithy version of his advice is when you are looking to expand your business, either use your existing products to get into new markets, or use your existing markets to diversify into new products. And be **VERY** careful when you find yourself doing both.

But if (a) you know what you're doing; (b) it makes strategic sense to go with new product **and** new clients; and (c) you're not averse to high risk, then, and only then, jump into a new market with a new product. But on your head be it!

Here's Ansoff's original model:

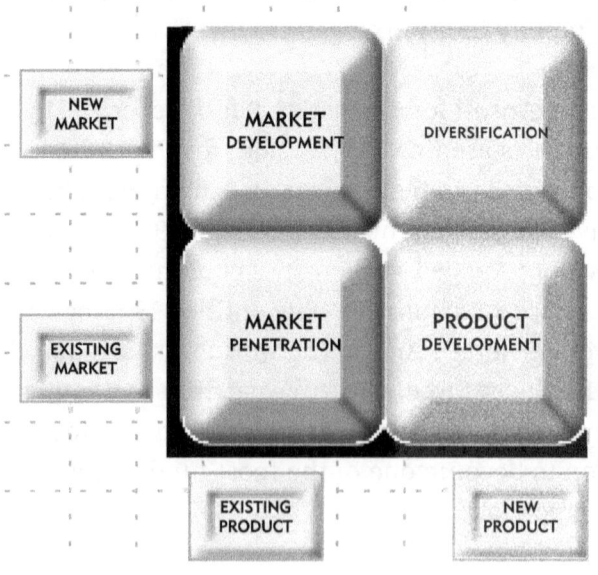

We've depicted it as a foursquare matrix because we both like the way a foursquare matrix plays out. However, Ansoff did not present his original tool as a matrix as he believed the top right hand square (diversification) was quite distinct and different from the other three strategic approaches.

Translating the four strategies, if you put more effort and energy into your **existing products and existing market**, as in the bottom left square, your strategic plan is one of grabbing more market share from your competition. So your action plan is about doing more of what you are essentially doing already.

If you **create a new product** for the market that you currently have and understand (the bottom right quadrant), you're staying firm on at least one area of knowledge and comfort and extending only your product development activities. You grow, but you minimise your risk.

If you keep your **existing products** but try to grow beyond your existing market into **new client areas** (top left square), then you lean on your existing product strength but add to your distribution channels, change the pricing or the packaging and undertake activities to attract new customers. This again minimises your risk.

The tricky one is when you decide, for whatever reasons are driving you, that the time is right to create a new product that you want to launch into a brand new market all in the same breath. Not for the faint-hearted! It's very risky as you are doing new things in new markets that you do not yet understand or have experience in.

Having said that, we're not averse to such a lack of caution. We referred earlier to the fact that you can't "create the future by fast-forwarding the past". Not in this day and age, anyway. There are numerous high profile individuals who have proved to the world the top right quadrant is the only way to go. How about the chap who started a record business in 1970, ignored all but the extreme "diversification" quadrant and by 1995, had added "airline", "publishing", "radio station", "soda drinks", "mobile phones" and "financial services" to his offering? You could ... but most of us wouldn't.

But then that's why Sir Richard Branson owns a Caribbean island and we don't.

PS: *Try applying the Ansoff matrix to your personal career. Instead of "market" use the words "my (existing) company" and replace "product" with "my job/role" or even "my skills".*

TAKE-OUT: When it comes to growing your company, be clear about how you want this to happen. For most small or large companies, year-on-year growth is about increasing market share within your established marketplace arena, using your existing products. Innovation largely is about changing the variables in a controlled way, either by opening up new distribution channels or by extending your product range. If you opt for radical diversification, make sure you are driven by the right reasons and the right reasoning!

▶▶ PITHY PLAN

- ▶▶ Create a foursquare matrix using the two primary components of your "market" and your "client".
- ▶▶ Populate the four squares with specific actions, events, products and plans.
- ▶▶ Use the graph to discuss the implications.
- ▶▶ Decide which quadrant or quadrants you need to focus on. It is unlikely that you will have the resources to do it all.

THINKING

Ockham's Razor

One of the more useful pieces of workplace wisdom comes from the unlikely source of a 14th century English friar. William of Ockham hailed from a small town (that's the Ockham bit) in the English county of Surrey. Remembered more for his skills as a logician than a man of the church, the law of parsimony and succinctness is attributed to him.

There was a whole lot of Latin involved in the original maxim so we'll skip straight along the timeline. 700 years later it is referred to as "Ockham's Razor" and translates roughly into "when you have two or more competing theories, the simplest one is probably the better option". And when you are trying to figure out something new,

I **knew** this razor cut would make it into history

you should *first* work with the components or elements that are already known.

Ockham used the principle to justify quite a few of his own philosophies and landed up having an unfortunate head-on with the Pope. This would have been distinctly career limiting to a lowly friar, but the phrase remains a useful piece of wisdom for business.

Ockham's Razor can mean a variety of things, depending on who is doing the speaking. For example, applying the Razor can become a way out of project conflict. If you have two people arguing against each other on the same subject or issue, the simplest one should be adopted ... *until some more evidence arises.* A lot of the time, the simplest explanation for something is probably the most accurate. Turn it around and you have the following advice: "The explanation requiring the fewest assumptions is most likely to be correct."

We're just wondering if it's legal to apply this to heated discussions between a man and wife? Now *that* could be interesting!

TAKE-OUT: Personally, we prefer to practise "lex parsimoniae" (the law of succinctness) and go with the "KISS" principle of **Keep It Simple ... Stupid!**

▸▸ PITHY PLAN

▸▸ Stumped for a clear path forward when faced with two opposing arguments or solutions? First step: Lay out all the facts.

▸▸ Cut out the excess and try to distil the two opposing possibilities down to their simplest forms.

▸▸ Work with what you have and know rather than try and make decisions based on what you don't know.

▸▸ Go with the solution that appears to be the most obvious and simplest. If you have to over-explain the proposal in ways that are difficult to understand, you might be heading along the wrong path.

▸▸ Once you've made your stand, go forward but check the facts and supporting information all along the road. Circumstances and decisions change.

THINKING

Palimpsest
Making New From Old

Business wisdom comes from all over if you tune in and notice it. One day, my disinclined-towards-business mother, Gloria, waved her paintbrushes over an old canvas she had dug up and exclaimed "Isn't Palimpsest simply fascinating!" Her definition of this was the overlaying of one work of art onto another in a way that produces a new piece of art completely - without losing the merits of the original. "Why face the daunting prospect of a blank canvas when you can start with something that already exists?" she explained.

What a perfectly pithy piece of business wisdom.

To be proper about things, palimpsest is normally in the context of working over old manuscript pages from a scroll or a book. In the pre-print era, writers and artists would often take existing works and scrape the original work off before using them again. And rarely was it a completely clean slate. So as to speak.

In the business world this is a great description for getting smart about inventing new things. No, we

> **PALIMPSEST**
>
> A parchment or tablet that has been written upon or inscribed two or three times, the previous text or texts having been imperfectly erased and remaining, therefore, still visible.
>
> Webster's New 20th Century Dictionary 2nd edition (Simon and Schuster) (From Greek palimpsestos: "Scraped again" meriam-webster.com)

haven't suddenly had a change of heart and are now advocating "fast-forwarding the past". We're simply suggesting that zero is not always the best starting point.

Let's say you come up with a really good idea or plan. Despite your conviction that it's a sure thing, it fails to get the green light. It doesn't get binned. It gets shelved. Three months or three years later, guess what - the environment has caught up and suddenly this mothballed solution ticks all the right boxes. In fact, you find someone else heavily engaged in the process of re-inventing the exact same thing you shelved all those months back. Time to take out the original old canvas and see what you can salvage. Change it.

Rub lots of it out. Clean the bits that don't work right off the page. Preserve the bits that still make sense.

If you know how to handle an Internet search engine, you know how to reach information on literally any subject under the sun. We're not suggesting you just copy other ideas but, in business, learning from what precedes and from what has happened already makes good sense. It's not plagiarism. It's smarter than that.

The mother of all examples in recent times must surely be the creation and launch of Facebook, that social networking phenomenon that has infiltrated our lives like a virus.

Despite the fact that you might only have got yourself acquainted with the concept of social networking once Facebook became big, it was by no means an original idea. If this was a history lesson, we would stop briefly at early forums, discussion groups, those very American college virtual reunion sites, even the first attempts of social sites like SixDegrees.com. But let's ignore all that and skip to 2002 when Friendster (a "virtual meeting site") was launched, followed shortly by LinkedIn (a networking business site), which today has over 30 million users. That same year MySpace was launched.

Facebook was not exactly based on an off-the-wall original idea. But then, that's the whole point. The founder/creator team, led by the contentious Mark Zukerberg, took an idea - launching in 2004 as a social networking site for Harvard students only, and then in 2006, into public domain - and turned it into the social networking juggernaut it has become.

Facebook now leads the global social networking pack. By far. There are more than 500 million active users (and by the time you read this, it'll be more) and more than 30 billion pieces of content - web links, posts, news, photographs - are shared every month. Of interest to the cell phone carrying South African market (92 out of every 100 South Africans have access to a cell phone according to the SA Institute of Race Relations) is that more than 200 million people access Facebook through their mobile phones.

Creativity does not necessarily start with an original thought. Today, if my team are struggling with a concept or an idea, I tell them to look it up. Go and see what others are doing. Get into the zone of your subject. Don't copy. Any fool can do that, but don't be truly foolish and re-invent the wheel. If you see something that works, adopt, adapt and make it work for your unique environment. You might not become a yuppie billionaire like Mark Zuckerberg (according to the Wall Street Journal, he adds US$ 112,3 million to his personal piggy bank every day), but you might just get that great business idea out off the shelf.

TAKE-OUT: Looking for a starting place? Don't stare at a blank piece of paper or a humming PC monitor in the hope that inspiration will strike you on the head. Get moving. Research, talk, interact, absorb. Open your eyes and look around you. And then improve on what you see.

▶▶ PITHY PLAN

- ▶▶ If you have an idea in your head, chances are there is something similar out there already. Get over it. Look hard and glean everything you can on the subject. Read. Watch. Google.

- ▶▶ Talk. Pick your audience but connect with people who might have some information between their ears that would prove/disprove/support or completely annihilate your plan. Take it on board. This is not a time to get stubborn.

- ▶▶ If you're still sure this is something that could fly, then adjust, tweak and update your plan to make it specific, innovative and unique.

THINKING

See Things as if for the First Time

The power of observation is underrated. We're all so busy Doing Things, we forget to stop and see what is right in front of us. We "see" through the filters and stereotypes our minds have built over the years. I have a favourite quote by Laurel Lee pinned up on my PC monitor as a daily reminder. "I know I am not seeing things as they are. I'm seeing things as I am."

When it comes to the business world, you simply cannot miss "seeing". Don't we just looove to categorise and label. We take comfort from boxing an event or a personality into something we recognise and that requires applying our existing filters. Those personal filters are subjective - can't change much about that, it's the way humans work - but it becomes dangerous when our own opinions, history, leanings and preconceptions kick in before we've had time to stand back and see things as they really are. Think about the colleagues around you. Can you remember your first instinctive impression of them? Your brain normally sees things correctly the first time. The challenge comes in trying to retain that insight

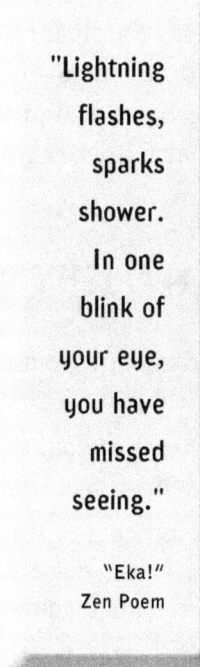

"Lightning flashes, sparks shower. In one blink of your eye, you have missed seeing."

"Eka!"
Zen Poem

months later when the layers of experience have pushed your original knowledge out of focus.

Friedrich Nietzsche, a 19th century German philosopher famously observed, "There are no facts, only interpretations." We're not going to dive into a deep and meaningful discussion about what reality is and is not but we are going to point out the relative impossibility of making decisions with a totally objective mind. Your values, attitudes, upbringing, education, likes, dislikes, life experiences and dare we say, biased opinions, might be the very stuff that make you an asset. But if you truly want to excel, recognise that you are seeing through those windows. Now take a giant step back and try looking at the same thing on the table as if you have never seen anything like it before.

TAKE OUT: Business opportunity on the table? Shaking hands with a stranger? Talking to a team-member you have known for years? Be aware of your personal filters. Seeing as if for the first time requires

conscious effort. Been around your company for a long time? Seen it all before? Have a closer look at some of those old ideas that didn't crack the nod the first time round. New technologies and processes might have come along that make it workable this time round.

▶▶ PITHY PLAN

- ▶▶ Pick a situation that would benefit from a "fresh pair of eyes" on the subject.
- ▶▶ If it's a proposal, put it in front of you. If it's a person, bring them to mind.
- ▶▶ Consciously go through the process of stepping away from what you know. This is not a time for outward activity. This is a mind game.
- ▶▶ Now read that document with attention to detail as if you have never seen it before. Keep the "new" mind approach as you do this and note your response.
- ▶▶ Go and find that person with whom you are having trouble. Look at them - really look at them - and listen to them as if this is the first time you have ever met them.
- ▶▶ This does require a conscious decision on your part to "let go". You might be surprised by what you observe.

THINKING

The DNA Test
- Do Not Assume

" But I *assumed* you knew ..."?

Those are the words you can expect to hear right before facing a management disaster of epic proportions.

The more you communicate detail and make sure everyone on the team knows all there is to know, the better chance you have of a smooth ride. When you work in a fast-moving operational environment, decisions are made on the hoof but even snappy decisions have to be made with a sensible array of facts. And if you really want to mess things up, you assume.

- "But I *thought* the client was on the same system as everyone else."
- "*Surely* it's up to the caterer to provide the serving plates too?"
- "Let's *assume* the current demand for CD's is going to continue for at least another fifteen years and go from there."

Prime Computer collared pole position for its banners. All was looking good ... until barcode technology not belonging to Prime had the runners' results in chaos.

It's the silly, small mistakes that bite the hardest and often those come about because someone along the chain has assumed knowledge of action rather than checking to see if the action has actually taken place.

Like the time a few years back when my PR company took our client, Prime Computer, to the Comrades. We pitched for and won the job of moving the then-mainly-manual timekeeping process to computers. It was a historic moment for everyone. In those days (we're talking early 80's) computers weren't the throw-em-on-the-backseat-of-your-car affairs we carry around today. We had to build air-conditioned huts to house the substantially sized "Supermini" computers, as they were so quaintly called back then, along with the paraphernalia (which was anything but portable or digital) that went along for the ride.

- ✔ Boxes and boxes of "continuous" computer paper: check;
- ✔ Spare parts for the computers: check;
- ✔ Integrated and what was then cutting-edge software that matched the runners with their personal and club details: check;
- ✔ An entire battalion of techies to look after above-mentioned computer and computer-stuff: check.

We had it all. Except the equipment to capture the runners' bar-coded race numbers as they staggered over the finish line. That job lay with Someone Else. And we assumed all would work well.

Hit the buzzer and watch the faces fall. The barcode machine packed up as runner 8017 crossed the line. Problem. There were another 3000 runners behind him. A save-the-day boy scout type magically conjured up several metres of fishing line and willing hands jumped to rip the paper numbers

> "Assumption is the mother of screw-up."
>
> Angelo Donghia
> (1935 - 1985)
> American designer

off the runners' t-shirts as they crossed the line, feeding them onto the fishing line while fast fingers manually captured times. Good plan. Except the fishing line broke, didn't it?

It turned into a trying day of red-faced runners, overwrought techies and accusing media.

Didn't do that again. The assumption bit, I mean. The Comrades we did do a few more times.

 **TAKE-OUT:** Check, ask, brief and inform. It's the only way everyone along the line delivers. "Do the DNA Test". This is one of those acronyms that work. We stick it up all over the office.

▶▶ PITHY PLAN

- ▶▶ Stick up notices roaring the warning "Do Not Assume"
- ▶▶ Make it a mantra, particularly within the ranks of your planners and project leaders. Teach them to check, recheck and check again that all the details are covered. When is too late ... it's too late

THINKING

Know What you Don't Know
(and know what you know)

For this pithy piece of wisdom, we thank you, Donald Rumsfeld. For those who don't watch CNN, Rumsfeld, erstwhile Defence Secretary of the United States, is one of those brilliant and deliciously outspoken figures of our time.

He was certainly durable, playing a role alongside presidents Robert Nixon, Gerald Ford, Ronald Reagan and George W. Bush. He was Defence Secretary at the time of the horrific 9/11 attacks.

He doesn't always say it succinctly but he does make it ... interesting.

Like the time he addressed a news briefing in early 2002 and came out with a real humdinger:

> "As we know, there are known knowns; there are things we know we know. We also know there are known unknowns; that is to say, we know there are some things we do not know. But there are also unknown unknowns - the ones we don't know we don't know."

You have to concentrate really hard to follow that. But there is some pithy savvy buried in all those words.

When faced with any decision, a good manager taps first into the knowledge he has in his head or at his fingertips. Dr Edward de Bono (he of the wonderful Six Hat Process) would call it *"The White Hat Process"*, which is about identifying and chalking up all the known facts before questioning the rest.

Then comes the obvious next step. What information is missing? The first step in figuring out obstacles and risks is to *anticipate* the unknown. An example for us was when Metropolitan was considering establishing a life insurance venture in India. Before we could make a strategic decision and long before we could leap into serious action, we had to face a string of "known unknowns". These included questions about how the potential Indian client differed from our (known!) South African; we needed to get a handle on our competition and what they were doing/not doing in the same country; we needed financial statistics about India and its market; and then there was the question of technology. What didn't we know about technology over there that would have an impact on possible cross-global link-ups? These were just some of the things on the list that we knew we had to grapple to the ground and turn into "known knowns".

But what about the stuff we don't know we don't know? This is what separates the good leaders from the ordinary. Don't ever get trapped under your own security blanket, secure in the knowledge that you've covered all your bases. Keep looking out for things you've missed or didn't even know were coming. As one of my cynical colleagues once said: "If you think that things are going well, you are obviously not in possession of all the facts".

TAKE-OUT: In any business situation, whether you're talking about a new business campaign, a project, introducing a new concept or reorganising a division, it's easy to apply what you know. It's also relatively easy to identify the information you are missing. But the real test of leadership is being alert to what you didn't see coming. Expect the unexpected.

▶▶ PITHY PLAN

- ▶▶ We like Edward de Bono's "Six Thinking Hats" process. It's never failed us, particularly in the realm of finding out what we don't know we don't know. Get people to talk and then write up the comments and stick them up on the wall or board as you go.

- ▶▶ The most important rule about this process is not to allow any blurring of the edges. You have to separate the areas of discussion. For example, if the conversation is green hat (exploring new ideas), nobody is allowed to put on the black hat and find fault. Don't allow anyone to offer opinions during the white hat session (facts only).

- ▶▶ In your project team or workshop group, facilitate and lead them through the following process of thinking while you record the comments and preferably put them up on the wall as you:

- **WHITE HAT:** Information that is either known already or needed. Stick strictly with the facts. Park the opinions.
- **YELLOW HAT:** This discussion is about the positive and optimistic aspects. Explore the potential "good stuff" for possible benefits.
- **BLACK HAT:** Here you explore why something might not work. Allow comments that are pessimistic. Let everyone get off their chest the things they don't like or they think could go wrong. People just love this one! Don't let it run rampant.
- **RED HAT:** This is about feelings, hunches, emotions and intuition.
- **GREEN HAT:** This is the creative hat. Encourage discussion about alternative approaches, possibilities, new ideas and concepts. All ideas are recorded. Do not allow anyone to sneak in black hat commentary!
- **BLUE HAT:** This is the hat used to manage the overall thinking process. It's the big picture element that normally allows for the handling of project management matters and control mechanisms.

Pithy Pearls

"Watch, listen, and learn. You can't know it all yourself. Anyone who thinks they do is destined for mediocrity."

Donald Trump
Business magnate, hotel and real estate developer

"If I had eight hours to chop down a tree, I'd spend six sharpening the axe."

Abraham Lincoln
16th President of the United States of America

"You can't overestimate the need to plan and prepare. In most of the mistakes I've made, there has been this common theme of inadequate planning beforehand. You really can't over-prepare in business!"

Chris Corrigan
Australian businessman

"They say a year in the Internet business is like a dog year - equivalent to seven years in a regular person's life. In other words, it's evolving faster and faster."

Vinton Cerf
American computer scientist,

DOING

"In life and business, there are two cardinal sins. The first is to act precipitously without thought and the second is to not act at all."

Carl Icahn
American financier and businessman

DOING

KYC –
Know Your Customer

It's become one of those catchy TLAs (Three Letter Acronyms) ever since the financial world went into overdrive to better regulate their approach to customer identification. KYC nowadays is the due diligence process banks perform to make sure they have a full handle on their customers but in the bigger business sense, "knowing your customer" is one of the most fundamental parts of any strategy.

Miss this and you mess up.

Sound so obvious it barely warrants the paper space? Here's a question for you, then: How many decisions about customers (in the field) are taken by people (in offices) who wouldn't know their *real* customer if he or she was literally dropped on their head? From our experience, a lot.

Psitek was a smart little South African company that hit on the idea of building portable telecommunications units that offered pay-by-the-minute conversations to remote areas of the country. They caught the wave

One of the spaza shops outside Cape Town that epitomises the new model. If you know WHAT your customer wants, all you have to do is place yourself WHERE the customer goes.

when the cell phone tsunami hit our shores. At the time, service providers were almost *mandated* to find ways of using the new technology to improve telecommunications in more remote communities in South Africa. Psitek was one of the new breed of technology companies that found the formula for making low-cost community phone booths a reality in areas that previously had no access to landline telecommunications. It was a hugely successful formula. For their follow-up act, Psitek partnered the

Before launching any new model, ask do you "Know Your Customer". And not what the research tells you on paper. You'll pick up very different information about your customer if you go into the field. Here colleague Maureen Mtoninshi moves in for a closer look.

mobile phone service providers and developed a little machine they called *Kazang* that made the dispensing of airtime vouchers possible from spaza shops, homes, taxi ranks and, frequently, from an upturned apple crate on a street corner. Customers wanted to buy their airtime vouchers and top-ups within easy walking distance of their home. Psitek delivered the solution. It was nifty and neat and offered some great micro-enterprise business opportunities. The challenge for the 10 000 or so vendors was to attract the local customer to their own sales outlet *away* from the nearest competition. In classic head office style, marketing was done by the marketing team... who sat in urban offices. The branding and material was brilliant and clever ... but most of the display boards despatched to the vendors landed up in, not on, the walls of the huts and spaza shops ... as building materials. Beautiful big posters might work in most cases but where do you stick or hang a poster in a 2 metre by 2 metre corrugated hut? Glossy leaflets gathered dust under the counter. Training brochures were sassy and user-friendly but in the end, word of mouth worked better with this audience. This market - and these customers - had rules of engagement that defied all traditional marketing text books.

One of the Kazang success stories we love is about an enterprising chap called Joe. Or *Bra* Joe as he is known by all. He's young, hip and happening and very entrepreneurial.From his home community in Soshanguve, a township north of Pretoria in Gauteng, Bra Joe has figured out a simple but effective formula. Don't sell products. Build an environment to attract the customer to you - in his case a place of entertainment - and then make your products available. No pressure. And with Bra Joe, it works. This clever young chap runs a vibey tavern as well as a community games and billiard room. Not surprisingly his main income

"Only in Africa"! Yup, we can all see the funny side of this unexpected - and definitely unplanned - use of national road signage but there lies a hint of a good lesson in this slice of real life. Marketing material, branding, product placement has to fit in with what works for the customer you have identified. Don't second-guess the response and behaviour. Know your customer.

is from the sale of liquor but on a busy Friday night, his little Kazang machine (among other things) hums just beautifully.

His formula was the instinctive understanding of what his community - and ultimately his customer - would respond to. No intellectual planning, no complicated analysis of marketing, no clever methods to dissect distribution models, not even any expensive marketing material... just a simple recognition of what will bring the feet in the direction of his small business.

TAKE-OUT: "KYC" is not simply a question of reading the research. And you certainly shouldn't make important client-related decisions from the remote sanctuary of your  office. Get down and dirty and walk a mile or three in your customers' shoes. When it comes to selling a product, sometimes you have to think laterally to create the optimum fertile selling ground.

▶▶ **PITHY PLAN**

- ▶▶ Start with the easily accessible research and facts about your customer.
- ▶▶ Now move into their world. Experience it. Ask them. Test your own understanding.
- ▶▶ Position your approach from the customer perspective, not from the viewpoint of the chaps who work in Process, Planning, Product development and Ops.

DOING

Carpe Diem
Don't Ask Permission – Seek Forgiveness

Isn't life marvellous? You invent an idea that is completely original, struggle to breathe life into the thing, write the documents, sweat through the logistics, lobby 'til your throat hurts and eventually see your brain-child take a few faltering steps into the world.

You've done it! It took you three years but success is finally yours. And you revel in the feeling ... right up until one of your previous critics (or even your boss?!) presents your idea - re-packaged and modified - but *your* idea, as the next big Strategic Project.
His Strategic Project.

Welcome to corporate reality. Actually, can that. Welcome to business reality. The demand to be first in this fast-changing world of technology has reached extremes. No sooner have you invented something in the privacy of your own head, then somebody somewhere launches the same thing and claims the territory.

There's a fine line between following the politics of lobbying and permission seeking and grabbing an idea you know is good and kicking life into the thing. Wimps disappear into the darkness of corporate corridors on a daily basis, howling in indignation as they do. No matter how great your thinking is, *it's nothing until it's delivered.*

We're not advocating you fly in the face of managerial hierarchy without so much as a backward glance but we are saying spit out your rubber teeth and grow real ones. Believe in an idea? So own it. Research, lobby, check your facts, bring on-board whoever you need to be your wingman (or your team or even your front man if necessary) but don't hover politely outside the boardroom door waiting for permission to enter.

> "Opportunities are like sunrises. If you wait too long you miss them."
>
> William Arthur Ward

Working harder means taking ownership and doing what is necessary to make the thing real. If it turns out to be the Great Idea you knew it to be, then the credit is yours to be grabbed. If it bombs, just remember your name is written all over it.
The responsibility of failure comes with the ownership.

Now for the cautionary. Nobody wants to employ a total renegade. There's a fine line between being proactive (in a good way) and arrogantly pushy (not in a good way). The first is a leader, the latter a problem. Corporate structures, with the various levels of responsibility and reporting modes, are created for a reason and normally they work. At the very least, try and keep the right people informed and involved without running for approval every time you edge forward. If your sixth sense warns you that you might be going a step too far, listen to it and embrace the permission process.

Pieter, the Do-it-Now member of Willem's early management team in the Information Technology division at Metropolitan, was known for his *interpretations* of the classics.

"As Shakespeare said, ..." he would boom out in one of his frequent team pep talks "He who taketh...haseth." No, the English poet and playwright never did write those words and Spell-Check threw them out of this document like dead fish but Pieter, never one to unnecessarily fetter a story with facts, loved the ring of the words.

You've probably been taught that grabbing in any way is impolite in polite circles. Conversely, "taking" can be seen as a show of strength in the business world.

Robin Williams as the English teacher John Keating in the brilliant movie, Dead Poet's Society, produced by Touchstone Pictures in association with Silver Screen Partners

We're not talking about grabbing the chocolate chip cookies off the boardroom table before everyone else. We're talking about jumping in with ownership where it's appropriate.

There is a Latin phrase that has been hauled off the dusty shelves of literary history and reinvented as a favourite modern-day maxim. In 1989 it became mainstream pithy pop-wisdom after Professor John Keating (*aka* actor Robin Williams - pictured here) urged his class of schoolboys in the still-brilliant movie "Dead Poet's Society".

"*Carpe Diem"* (Seize the day). Make your lives extraordinary."

In business terms, it means don't get so paranoid about the future and the "What If" scenario planning that you lose what is right in front of you.

In business, now more than ever, you have to cast your eye towards the future. You have to worry about environmental matters, shifting economic models, new competition lurking around the corner, a change in marketplace, a complete shift in trend ... but at the end of the day, you make your mark in the here and now.

People also judge you by what you do in the here and now. They see evidence of results today. And the future is largely dependent on how you handle the current.

TAKE-OUT: Being a leader or a successful entrepreneur, as opposed to being owner of an *almost* successful business, is about doing something. It's about having the right ideas but it's also about having the gumption to deliver. Sometimes that means taking a risk. As Yoda, the Jedi Master in the movie *Star Wars* so famously said: 'Do or do not. There is no try."

Asking permission might be the right thing to do but seeking forgiveness later might be the *best* thing to do.

▶▶ PITHY PLAN

▶▶ Be sure about what you're about to do. If it's a whimsical idea you haven't checked out or researched, then we suggest you do a bit of both.

▶▶ Sure? Okay, now get into action. Don't go so far that you risk your entire job and can't retreat, but start the process. The kind of thing you could kick into action:

> ▶ Do the research and write a recommendation. Give it to the right people.

> ▶ Do a mini-pilot or test within your own team or within an area you can influence.
> Manage it tightly. Measure and monitor.
> If you get the results, now you have ammunition to take the next step - and results are so much more effective than talking through a vague idea.

▶▶ Take it to the next level. Use what you've done to effect the proper next step.

▶▶ Keep a careful eye on all around you. Include those you think appropriate, or career-savvy to include. Not everyone is going to love the fact that you've already gone "out there" with some action.

▶▶ And don't tell anybody about it unless you have to. That's not for conspiratorial reasons. It's for self-preservation.

DOING

Authority is Never Given – *It is taken*

As a rule, you would think of "authority" as being The Boss. He (or she) who must be obeyed. In this context, we regard "authority" as being less about position and more about how you handle yourself and step up to the plate when the opportunity presents itself.

"But Management won't let me..."

"Management should do something about this ..."

And our favourite, said with an air of justification and finality, "I'm going to escalate it upwards. That will sort this out."

How easy life is for us as children. At school the teacher decides everything for our son, Ryan. He is told when to drink his tea-break juice and where to stand in the queue for Friday morning assembly. He has his "project deliverables" for the week written into his homework book and the method of measurement - hand scribbled smiley faces and frowning faces - is unequivocal.
At school, Ryan obeys authority and rests easy in that.

(At home, he is authority. Willem erected a sign outside our house shortly after he was born: "Under New Management." The sign is still hanging.) When he's in a tight spot, he rests in the knowledge that he can manage upwards. His teacher will show him the next step. That's what teachers are there for.

If Ryan were to join a company when he grows up, I will strongly advise him against switching his dependency from his teacher to his manager. It's not for management to make him happy. It's not even for management to push him up the grades and send him on training courses. It **is** for management to provide the tools and opportunities to get the job done. The rest will be up to Ryan.

Managers are not accountable for every small part of their employee's lives or their careers. It's an onerous and thankless burden. Hire the right person, give them the job, the responsibilities, the training and the resources. And then you can give them the authority to act. But it only becomes real if that authority is actually taken and the accountabilities accepted.

"I can't get approval from Humbert Higgins subsidiary to upgrade their switchboard even though the business case makes it clear that we need to," whined one junior manager to Willem one day. "I'm sick of it. We've been trying to sort this one out for 12 months."

"And what would you do if you were management?"

The young man looked at his boss sceptically, suspecting a trick question. "Me?"

"You."

This junior manager had just attempted a classic upward delegation manoeuvre and was about to brush his hands off with a sense of accomplishment. It certainly wasn't supposed to come back at him.

"I would go to Humbert Higgins and persuade them to run a small pilot with our help to prove the business case before getting the order from them to upgrade their whole national switchboard," he said eventually.

"What do you need to do it?" asked Willem.

"R150 000." Hesitation. "Maybe R200 000".

"You've got it. You could have asked for this before. So now take it and run with it. But I want measurable results."

"Me?"

"You."

The young manager got his money, did the pilot, got the results and eventually launched the national upgrade of Humbert Higgins' switchboard. He also put in place the most thorough testing process he'd ever masterminded. He had to. Not only had he taken the authority, but also the accountability that came along with it. *(True story. Names have been changed to preserve the pride of our chief role-players who would deny all memory of the story!)*

 **TAKE-OUT:** If you are a manager, don't mistake your job for having to be the one who decides on every

single detail. Empowerment is one of the most liberating qualities of good management. If you are aspiring to be the manager, stop delegating upwards. Do your homework, earn the responsibility of leadership and motivate to take on the accountability. That's if you *want* to grow up the management ladder.

▸▸ PITHY PLAN

- ▸▸ When you're the one who has been given the task, ensure that you have the necessary authority to execute the task. Then **exercise** that authority when necessary to get the job done.
- ▸▸ When you're the one giving someone else a task to do, make sure they have the necessary authority to execute the task. Ensure that they understand their authority. Do they need even more authority to do the job? No? Good.
That's the point when they must take full accountability for the task and deliver. No excuses. No upward delegation.

DOING

Don't Confuse Activity With Results

A wise man once said, "When you don't know your destination, any route will do." Or to quote an Ashanti proverb: "If you are on the road to nowhere, find another road." Neither is applaudable in the business world.

One of the easiest things in the world is to look busy. In fact, you can legitimately *be* busy. But if the goal is not reached or the desired outcome not happening, why bother? You might as well choose a book and go and sit in the company parking lot.

Activity should be measured according to results, not according to the process you took to get there. Having said that, you have to be crystal clear about your end result.

How often have you sat in one of those weekly Operations Meetings and listened to team-members as they prattle happily about all their busy activity during the week-that-was? That's nice to know but what really matters is this: "What have you actually achieved?"

If you have a team you can trust with clear deliverables that you have mutually agreed on and with the promise of appropriate reward on successful delivery, try a whole new way of managing them. Judge and praise them according to output rather than length of time bums are in their swivel seats. Of course, you can't run an empty shop. Appealing though it sounds, you can't always have a virtual environment with everyone "working from home".

However, there may be legitimate and rational merit to have the work done outside of conventional office times and away from the office environment. Just make clear the rules, the timing, the objectives and the hard deliverables.

We had that situation with a big catering client recently. Everybody wanted to work from home and because this was a hip, hop and happening young company, management

> *"Where most of us end up there is no knowing, but the hell-bent get where they are going."*
>
> James Thurber

thought it was very forward thinking to embrace the virtual office model. So we devised a four square matrix. (They work every time!)

The axes were pretty straightforward. We asked two questions:

1. **Can the work you do be measured easily?**

    If I was designing the website for the company, my measurement is based on the web site itself. Measureable. Case closed. If I was making cakes for a coffee shop, my output isn't just measureable, it's edible. Not all the employees in this company did work that was quite so tangible, which made it tricky for management to keep tabs on them, measure their contribution and reward accordingly.

2. **Can you carry out your job without (i) tapping into company resources (such as PC's, systems or kitchens) OR (ii) the need to interact regularly with other team members inside the offices?**

If there was a question mark over either of these issues, it was clear that "working from home" could be problematic.

It was an easy matrix to follow and took away all the emotion from deciding who should pull up a seat and get working and who could head for virtual working territory.

TAKE-OUT: Activity is not the same as results. Beware of a smooth-talking team member who mops her brow and talks loudly about how busy she's been.

Any fool can create "To Do" lists. What you want is results. It is not what you do that matters, it is what you achieve.

▶▶ PITHY PLAN

- ▶▶ As a manager, encourage feedback on results, not activities.
- ▶▶ Acknowledge the blood, sweat and tears that has gone into the activity, but don't make it a cause for national celebration.
- ▶▶ Measure and reward the right things and agree to these upfront.
- ▶▶ Get your team to write their performance plans based on achievements instead of hours spent behind the desk or in the field.
- ▶▶ It's all a matter of attitude

DOING

Don't Confuse Quality *with Perfection*

Quality is fine but perfection is better. Right? ... Wrong! When it comes to the business world, perfection could turn out to be your downfall. Over the years, we have seen people struggle to perfect a document, sometimes taking days out of their diary. It's good to reach for excellence but when is too much perfection ... too much? We say it's a simple rule of mutual understanding and expectation. When the job is done in a way that the client is pleased as punch and signs off, then the job is done. Finish.

But we just can't leave it at that, can we? There is a part inside of us that has to go back and fiddle. We have to go back and back again.

Willem and I have a designer-builder who has been part of the ever-evolving place we call home for some years now. He is unusual. Technically proficient and experienced in all elements of the building profession, Colin sees life through the eyes of an artist. He'd have built the Sistine Chapel *and* painted it in another life. But Colin is a perfectionist, a rare species in the construction industry. Good-enough is never good enough for Colin. Long after we have admired a new cupboard, applauded the finish on a new door, whistled through our teeth over the smooth finish of a tiled floor ... *and agreed that the job is finished* ... we find Colin ripping up his creation.

"It's not quite right," he mutters.

We've "signed off". We're ready to pay. But still our perfectionist builder friend returns to the finished job once, if not twice, again. As the client, we gain from this zeal for perfection but in the business world, perfection has serious restrictions.

One of the most gifted graphic designers I know is our friend Claire. Creating symmetry and beauty out of random components such as pictures and text is what Claire does best. During our years of working together in the publishing industry, we created a roomful of magazines, trade journals, newspapers and niche market trade books. When it came to the aesthetics of layout, no one can touch her. The thing about Claire though is that she is a perfectionist. We faced many a deadline together and many a sleepless night. (In the design world, the two go hand-in-hand.) By 3.00 am I would be looking at quality layouts, enthusiastically congratulating ourselves on getting the job done. Claire would stare at the same page in misery.

"No! It's not *quite* right."

She would trim the converging lines on her page layout with the concentration of a geologist aligning the latitudes and longitudes of our planet.

And the clock would tick on by. Long after our client would have eagerly signed off on a job well done, Claire is back at her desk, "just fixing" this and "tweaking" that.

When the job is good enough, it's good enough. Leave it and move on to the next thing. This gives you a better handle on time management and an improved ability to rise above the noise level of detail and see the important big picture.

Ask yourself: Does the thing you have created do the job really well or is there something else you need to *take away* in order to make it better? Nowhere does this apply more aptly than to the masterminding of documents. Some people just can't leave well alone.

> "Perfection is achieved, not when there is nothing more to add but when there is nothing left to take away."
>
> Antoine de Saint-Exupery

Calista Flockhart as Ally McBeal in the American hit series of the same name; produced by David E. Kelley

When the document explains what you need to explain in a way that your audience properly understands it, then stop fiddling and seal the envelope. Or hit "send".

Perfection is a daunting objective. It's not that it's unachievable. It's just that it is seldom necessary. You're not trying to build an edifice for generations to come. You're aiming for the kind of quality that meets the client's requirements.

There was a successful television show that hit all the big-time ratings from 1997 to 2002. (Anyone else out there remember Ally MacBeal?). A line from that show is a warning about life:

"Sometimes ... when you hold out for everything, you walk away with nothing."

TAKE-OUT: Never stint on quality. But when the job is done, the job is done. Taking it to your personal view of perfection is neither productive nor rewarding for you or your company. Quality is achieved when the client's requirements are met. Anything more is wasted effort. Anything less will result in a dissatisfied client.

▶▶ PITHY PLAN

- ▶▶ Negotiate upfront the details of what needs to be done and by when.
- ▶▶ Determine when the client (or boss) will be happy with a job done.
- ▶▶ Make sure all boxes are checked on that agreement before considering it complete and then hand it over. As complete.
- ▶▶ Now move onto the next job. Go on. You can do it.

DOING

Brake Into the Corner, *Accelerate Out*

Driving didn't come easily to me. Frankly I was terrified of the whole idea. Don't ask me why. Maybe it had something to do with the shock of emigrating from the taxis and traffic of London, England to the taxis and traffic of East London, South Africa. I just know that I turned 18 without so much as applying for a learner's. Then I crossed 21, graduated and got an editorial job. Suddenly I *needed* to travel just to do my work. This was pre-email era, remember. And I even mean pre-digital. Despite the fact that Alexander Bain had invented fax machines as far back as 1843, this now antediluvian piece of technology had not yet hit the standard office-equipment lists during the 80's. Suddenly I found myself in dire need of (a) a car and (b) a driving licence. Preferably not in that order.

My brother Nigel took me in hand. Three years younger than I am, he, of course, got his learner's licence 24 nano-seconds after he crossed 18. Bicycling, surfing, boating, driving ... those were his things. His method for getting me over my fear of driving was simple.

Terrify me further. He sneakily navigated his Learner-Sister "by mistake" onto Durban's M1 highway at peak traffic time and then sat back as I grappled with the fight-or-flight components of my brain. Let's just say some sibling relationship repair work had to be done after that. But his method worked. I broke the fear barrier. The lesson I remember the most from that day was the principle of cornering.

"Brake into the corner", he encouraged quietly, ignoring the fact that my knuckles were turning white on the steering wheel. "Accelerate out."

Like all good advice and truisms, it is painfully obvious. Once you know it.

12 months later, I hit my first professional publishing crisis at a company called Group Editors (*a tour de*

force publishing house and public relations company in its time that has long since disappeared). Critical photo images had gone missing for a major annual report job. The instinct is to panic and reach for a brown paper bag. "Brake into the corner". The words popped into my brain like a pre-programmed auto-response. I stopped the whole production process for a brief time-out as we thought things through carefully. The solution: I got in my car (I told you e-mails hadn't been invented yet) and drove to the client's head-office archive department where I sifted through 30 enormous boxes of stored photographs (no, not electronic. I thought we had straightened that out) and found a different batch of images that did just fine. By this stage the production presses were panting so we didn't accelerate out of the corner. We burned rubber. It was a little mantra I was to use countless times in the years ahead.

In philosophy, they refer to it as The Pause. It's a conscious awareness on your part to let go and breathe for a moment before making the next decision, moving out the next action or just saying the next words. Don't fill that moment with activities. Don't even think. Just tune in for a minute.

So obvious. So simple. So true.
Thanks, Brother!

TAKE-OUT: As busy people of the 21st century, we've accepted perpetual motion as *de facto*. Even when we're taking a time-out, our fingers are either working cell phones or palm computers. What's more, we *reward* people for being in perpetual motion! Learn that stopping - just for a moment - to check on status quo can be time best spent.

▶▶ PITHY PLAN

- ▶▶ When faced with a crisis or a difficult corner to navigate in a project or task, put both hands on "the wheel" and brake into your corner.
- ▶▶ Check. Think. Ask. Check again.
- ▶▶ Once you're comfortable with the way forward and you know what to do, don't waste time dilly-dallying around. Put foot and pick up speed again. Accelerate out and onward.

DOING

Don't take the Monkey
On Your Back

Cartoon: William Oncken Corporation

Depending on which book you study, this expression can mean a variety of things. We'll leave the obvious one alone and assume you don't work for a circus. Flipping back through history, at different times it meant different things. At a stretch, it could be a reference to your superior intelligence. Drawing from slightly less ancient history, it could mean you are slightly mad or even overly obsessed with something.

Within the modern working world, it has come to mean you're the sucker who is taking on all the work. In 1974, the Harvard Business Review published an article entitled *"Management Time: Who's Got the Monkey?"* by William Oncken and Donald L Wass.

It was one of those classic pieces of business wisdom that gave birth to a new catch phrase as well as waves of seminars, books and articles on the subject.

When do you have the monkey on your back? When you're daft enough to accept primary responsibility for someone else's responsibilities or tasks, thereby transferring "the monkey" from his or her back to yours.

And it might not be your intended action. Think carefully before you step in with any one of these comments: *"Maybe I can give it some thought before you proceed?"*, *"Let me check on that before you do the presentation"*, *"I'll add in some comments on your document before you finish the draft"*. You just shifted the monkey - and the responsibility for re-igniting active status - onto your back.

TAKE-OUT: Watch your back! Guide but don't take on the responsibility. "I'll give you an outline for you to follow" means you've taken the monkey onto your back. By contrast "Do the document and then show me before presenting to the board" is effective delegation. Be careful about letting go completely. "Do the presentation and let me know how it went" is abdication. There is a difference between encouraging self-empowerment and risking your own job.

▶▶ PITHY PLAN

- ▶▶ During any event, project or programme, deciding ownership of roles and responsibilities is a fundamental step.
- ▶▶ Ensure there is clarity as to how far that responsibility extends i.e. what is included and what is excluded.
- ▶▶ As the "doing" person in this agreement, understand that this particular monkey is yours. Take it. Feed it. Guard it. Keep it alive. Own it.
- ▶▶ As a manager or even as a peer person in the division, play your part but don't say or do things that effectively have the monkey come home with you.
- ▶▶ And if you do make this move ... understand the implication. The monkey is now all yours.

Pithy Pearls

"I have been impressed by the urgency of doing. Knowing is not enough; we must apply. Being willing is not enough; we must do."

Leonardo da Vinci
Italian painter, sculptor, architect, inventor

"To do two things at once is to do neither."

Publilius Syrus
1st century Latin writer

"I think that I have just remembered something I forgot to do yesterday and shan't be able to do tomorrow. So I suppose I really ought to go back and do it now."

Piglet in "Winnie the Pooh" by A.A.Milne

"Those who make the worst use of their time are the first to complain of its brevity."

Jean de la Bryere
17th century French writer and novelist

"Never mistake motion for action."

Ernest Hemingway
American writer and journalist

Pithy Pearls

"Ability is what you're capable of doing. Motivation determines what you do. Attitude determines how you do it."

Lou Holtz
American Football Coach

"The world is not dangerous because of those who do harm but because of those who look at it without doing anything."

Albert Einstein
American Physicist

"Wisdom is knowing what to do next, skill is know how to do it, and virtue is doing it."

David Starr Jordon
American ichthyologist and educator

"Never interrupt someone doing what you said couldn't be done."

Amelia Earhart
pilot

"Let everything you do be done as if it makes a difference."

William James
American psychologist and philosopher

LEADING

"Pull the string, and it will follow wherever you wish. Push it, and it will nowhere at all."

Dwight D. Eisenhower

Supreme Commander of the Allied Forces WW2 and President of USA 1953-1961[M2]

LEADING

Wherever My People Go, I must follow *(For I am their leader)*

I first saw these words on a piece of paper, stuck almost defiantly to the wall in the office of the managing director of a steel manufacturing company. It's a wonderful approach as long as you know that the important word is *lead*, not *follow*.

Leading from the front is a more obvious way to do things. If you're the guy in charge then you had better make sure you are seen as that ... hence our choice of a quotation from Eisenhower on the previous page. People like strong, visible leadership. However, a confident leader doesn't necessarily have to lead from front stage and centre. Sometimes the best approach to effective management is literally to lead from behind.

A good manager gives his - or her - team members enough knowledge, skills, training, teaching, mentoring, parameters, instructions and authority to run their own areas of responsibility ... and then the manager steps back. There is nothing worse than a manager whose sole reason for being is to check on the progress of his report-ins ... *every half hour*. This kind of manager either has a highly elevated need for control or he is lacking in self-worth.

Surely, if you have employed and mentored the right team in the first place, they can deliver. And the more they deliver (without you interfering with advanced forms of micro-management), the better you look. Reflected praise sits very well on the shoulders of a strong leader.

Never take your eyes off the ball. Never stop keeping your ears open. Never stop talking or demanding feedback. Never close your office door to requests for help and guidance. We're talking delegation not abdication.

Good managers do not lead noisily from the front of the bus nor do they have the inclination to do so.

There is nothing more rewarding than watching a member of your team grab an idea and start running with it as if they had invented the thing. It doesn't matter if you are the one who thought it up in the first place. Sow the seed and watch someone below you take ownership. You'll be more sure of successful delivery than if you had given them the job of executing the idea on your behalf.

And while we are on the subject of leadership - a thought worth remembering is to never lead so far in front that your people (or your clients for that matter) lose sight of you. You might enjoy the sheer glory of being brilliant, innovative and ahead of your time in thinking, but if you are so far ahead of those whom you are leading, it will be a solitary victory.

TAKE-OUT: Weak leaders have to let the world know they are the real powerhouses by taking centre-stage all the time. Great leaders apply skills of superb mentorship and allow their team members to stretch and grow.

Of course this, in turn, reflects on the leader.

▶▶ PITHY PLAN

- ▶▶ Make sure you know what kind of leader you are.

- ▶▶ If you want to mentor and lead your team or staff members to greatness, be strong in your role and clear in your directives, but don't stand in front of the bandstand and micro-manage.

  - ▶ If you want to lead noisily from the front of the bus, then go ahead. It's a style of leadership that will no doubt ensure obedience and results but it's not a style to bring about growth in those who report into you.

  - ▶ Now make sure those around you understand which of the two leadership styles you use. Each has its own set of rules.

LEADING

Don't Dither. Decide.

We both started our careers back in the technological dark ages. All right, so it was only the seventies. But it was all very last century. In so many ways.

We thought it was fast then. Quotations were typed, painfully, onto sheets of paper and *hand-delivered* to the client. That meant jumping into your car, or having a really good relationship with the company deliveryman. You could only have telephone conversations with people at home or in the office. That's where telephones were back then. If you wanted to engage in a written conversation, it could take weeks. You write. You post. They read. They write. They post. You read. You write ... you get the gist.

Research? That involved hours in your local library where books were still made of paper. Search engines? Of course we had search engines. They were those little robotic vehicles made out of Sunday Roast tin foil that were used to explore the moon.

And Googling was not a concept, let alone a verb.

Where we're going with this, is decision-making. Back then, a decision was a decision. Plans had the phrase "10-Year" written before them. Decisions took months to make and even more months to undo. That was all before the digital age where businesses are bought and sold at the click of a mouse.

Nobody is going to give you a Noddy Badge for snap decisions that create havoc and result in the wrong outcome ... but you do need to get with the programme and realise everything has speeded up. Including decisions. And these days the race is on. In the USA, Bell Laboratories pioneered the mobile phone and kicked out their trial run pilot projects in 1979. By 1983, they had opened their first public service. Impressive. Speedy. But, *in the meanwhile*, the Scandinavians fast-forwarded their own go-live date and hit the market running in 1981. Not every product

> "It is a terrible thing to look over your shoulder when you are trying to lead - and find no-one there."
>
> Franklin D. Roosevelt

Decision making - anytime, anyplace. Even Mumbai Airport.

launch needs to be first-to-market but, in the fierce game of technology, first is often pole position.

The answer lies in balance. The 21st century manager has to be fleet of foot but careful to make the *right* decisions. Study everything you have in front of you. Listen to your warriors and report-ins (presuming you employed the right ones in the first place)

> **I pointed out to you the stars and all you saw was the tip of my finger.**
>
> (African Proverb)

but then make a decision. The decision you make at that time might not be the best decision overall but it will probably be the right decision for that moment. Of course there's a catch. You can't sit back on your laurels and reward yourself with three straight weeks of playing golf. You have to keep an eye on your decision - and its repercussions - and adjust the action in play where necessary.

You've heard the expression "paralysis by analysis"? H. Igor Ansoff, whom we talked about earlier, is credited with coming up with this pithy little phrase. He was concerned that managers would be so caught up in the models - including his own marketing tool - that they would never progress to making a decision and acting on it. We're saying the same thing here. Don't get caught up in your own decision-making process to the point that you either don't make a decision at all, or agonise so long that everyone has left the building. And your competition moved in.

TAKE-OUT: You're paid the big bucks to make decisions. Fine. But don't drown in your own self-importance. Today's leaders are swift in decision-making and prepared to adjust - within reason and budget - where necessary. You can only make your decisions on what you have and know now.

▶▶ PITHY PLAN

- ▶▶ A lot of leaders are made by how they behave rather than what they do.
- ▶▶ If you dither, people might see it as a sign of uncertainty, even weakness.
- ▶▶ As long as you're working off a base of knowledge, intelligence and common sense, make decisions with an air of confidence. Seldom in life will you have the full information at your fingertips. Go with what you have.
- ▶▶ Better to adjust the sails as you go than never leave the harbour.

LEADING

"Skip-Level" Meetings
(Talk to the Troops, Not Just Your Report-Ins)

"So how many tea-cloths do *you* think we need this year?"

Silly, inconsequential question in the life of a busy manager? Maybe, but not to the lady who has handled the tea cloths every day of her life during 27 years of dedicated service. And it is that same lady who will have an idea or two of her own to make her area more efficient and more productive. Everything in life is relative.

Beware the traditional pyramid of corporate ladders. If you're not careful, you'll build yourself an ivory tower so far away from the foot soldiers you wouldn't even know if a war was about to start up on your own frontiers.

Talk to the troops.

All of them.

A small initiative such as Skip-Level Meetings can pay great dividends. The trouble with only ever talking to

your direct report-ins is that you only get to see the world *they* paint for you. And that might not be the real picture. Leaping over the traditional lines of management, book random informal sessions with members of staff at any level except those who report into you. Lay down a few rules of engagement.
We suggest you ban all whining or complaining that is thrown at you without a good positive solution.
We also strongly advise that you place a further ban on tale telling about their own managers. And NEVER talk about their job grade! There are other processes and far more appropriate mechanisms to deal with that.

During these chats, kick-off with some "getting to know you" small talk but try asking everyone the same specific question: *If you ran your department, what would you do differently?*

Some of the ladies who work in the canteen at Metropolitan Life.

> "Some men succeed by what they know; some by what they do; and a few by what they are."
>
> Elbert Hubbard
> American writer and philosopher

You might land up rethinking your strategy to trash one of those expensive projects embarked upon last year. Or you may just be ordering an extra five tea cloths.

TAKE-OUT: Even in the most modern of 21st century businesses, we fall back on old hierarchical structure habits. Top management talks to middle management who delegates to lower management who manages "The Rest". You'd be surprised what can be learned by skipping a few levels and having a conversation outside traditional report-in structures about what is really happening down there.

▶▶ **PITHY PLAN**

- ▶▶ Every few months or so, set aside time for "Skip Level" Meetings. Introduce the concept as common knowledge. Let your staff or team members know that "their turn" will come. Half the value of this exercise lies in making our desire to meet with - and listen to - all rank and file public knowledge.
- ▶▶ These are informal meetings, not workshops. Keep them short and pleasant.
- ▶▶ Ask the person general questions about their job to keep things relaxed and then toss in a few questions that could really make a difference to you as a leader.

We like:
  - ▶ "If you were the manager of your section, what changes would you make right now?
  - ▶ "If there was one thing you would change about the way this company is run, what would that thing be?"

LEADING

Job on the (Time) Line

One management responsibility that is easy to get wrong is the structuring of people resources. Do you group everyone according to the way the company is structured? What about structuring according to skill sets? Or process flow?

During the mid-nineties, Willem was IT Executive for Anglo American Corporation. At one extreme end of the IT division's timeline, service delivery demanded a swift turnaround of between two and four hours. We're talking call centres, help desks, trouble-shooters, complaints handling and essential IT and desktop maintenance. At the other end of the scale, timelines for strategic initiatives and certain macro-projects could peg a delivery date of six months to a year, if not longer. Between the two extremes were different turnaround demands ranging from a few working days to several weeks.

The solution he applied was to match his individual managers to appropriate areas of responsibility using timeline logic. Each manager and service area was organised according to the different timelines of service delivery, which were then matched to the essential personality traits and strengths of the individual managers.

The matching of service environment to personality types is an essential step in the process. If you were managing an athletics team, you wouldn't ask sprinter World Record holder Usain Bolt to compete in the next Comrades Marathon, would you? And Zimbabwean Stephen Muzhingi, who won the gruelling 90km ultra marathon in 2009 and 2010, would probably run a mile, if you pardon the pun, at the idea of a 100m sprint.

Take that sports lovers!

Photo: www.askmen.com

Usain Bolt: living legend of the athletics world. He took top honours at both the 2008 Beijing Olympics and the 2012 London Olympics. Officially the fastest man on earth!

Photo: Sowetan

Stephen Muzhingi wins the 2010 Comrades Marathon for the second year in a row.

So would your fast-thinking organisational champion, whose speciality is an incredible coping mechanism for crises, be best suited to big picture strategising that requires a fair amount of long term crystal ball gazing? Probably not. Of course, a good manager would have to deal with both extreme ends of the spectrum but a little lower down the ranks. It's a big stretch to successfully manage both on a daily basis.

When Willem took over the technology division of Metropolitan, the two personalities at either end of the timeline extremes had an obvious match. Jan, an erstwhile IT "techie" supremo with a real love of applying technology to Big Picture thinking, would get *really* excited when asked to think into the future. The fact that the ultimate deliverables were three to five years from each planning stage was not a deterrent. If anything it was a motivator. Bringing the future towards the present was Jan's personal view of Willy Wonka entering the chocolate factory. He was perfect for running the strategic innovation environment.

By contrast, Pieter, the management team's "do it now" champion, would have found that a job from hell. As far as he was concerned, tomorrow was an excuse for things that should have been accomplished today. Pieter literally churned the air up around him as he faced problems head on, not resting until the thing was solved. He was ideal for the short end of the timeline.

> *P.S. Legend has it that Pieter continued with his particular management style into retirement. Even his garden was subjected to his critical operational eye. A new bed of lettuce was quickly sorted into "performers" and "non-performers". The hapless under-developed and under-achieving leaves were punished with the severest of disciplinary methods - they were uprooted and left to wither.*

 **TAKE-OUT:** A good manager is a good manager. But when your structure and the responsibility are matched to the personality types of your managers, the results are always improved.

▶▶ PITHY PLAN

- ▶▶ Group the tasks and outputs handled by your division into bundles depending on their respective timeline zones. Ask yourself what timing you expect for each specific group of responsibilities.

- ▶▶ Consider the personality-type and profile of your leaders and managers. Be careful. This requires complete clarity and objectivity.

- ▶▶ Now put the right manager in charge of a bundle that operates in a timezone that matches his or her inherent personality.

- ▶▶ Now write and tell us about how that worked out for you!

LEADING

Don't Bring Me Problems
Bring Me Solutions

She's sitting in front of you with a ream of paper heavier than your chair. She's done her research and got an answer for every statistic you throw her way. You're listening attentively so she's on a roll.

"Now you see why we have been experiencing this downtime problem over the past 18 months. It is *entirely* the fault of the Y9-Triple K team over in Dep Tech."

This was pretty much as it played out at Anglo American one day in Willem's office. There are people who see the problems. And then there are people who see the problem and take it upon themselves to think up a solution. In this particular case, he decided to teach his staff member a little lesson. "So what's your recommendation?"

She looked at him blankly. "That's not my job."

If ever there is a hot button for Willem, it's those four words. "But your area is experiencing problems as a result of this downtime."

"Yes, and the Y9-Triple K team must fix it."

"And what is *your* recommendation?"

"If Management would just look at the statistics ..."

"When you have a solution ... as well as all the statistics ... come and see me again."

Everyone's a critic. It's easy to gather data and point a finger. You can even justify it by showing where it's affecting your own team. But the leaders are the individuals who see the problem, assess, analyse and then suggest a better solution. Willem has a rule. Bring me the problem by all means but make sure you have a solution lined up. It doesn't have to be *the* solution but don't attempt this conversation without *any* solution. At least it shows you have thought about it.

TAKE-OUT: We can all get a rugby team to win the World Cup when we are the all-knowing, invincible coach, directing the players from the safety of our favourite television chair. Anyone can criticise but if you want to be noticed, bring the problem and a possible solution to the table. And if you're the leader, don't tolerate whinge sessions if there isn't a positive suggestion and solution coming out of the conversation.

▶▶ PITHY PLAN

- ▶▶ If you aspire to management, this is the stuff that gets you noticed!
  - ▶ If you spot a problem, make sure you have a solution well-worked out before you approach your superiors with your little mission of tattle-taleing or reporting.
  - ▶ It must be thought-through, sensible, appropriate and feasible.
  - ▶ It doesn't have to be the solution.
- ▶▶ If you are management:
  - ▶ Don't allow upward delegation to you without transferring some, if not all, of the ownership back. This is a growth opportunity for them. Make it a rule that a problem brought to your attention must be accompanied by a solution.
  - ▶ It must be thought-through, sensible, appropriate and feasible.
  - ▶ It doesn't have to be the solution.

LEADING

Don't tell me what you can't do. Tell me what you can do

Leading in with a negative is a no-no.

It's one of the cardinal sins and yet we hear it everywhere - board meetings, training rooms, presentations, public speeches and most frequently of all, in call centres. "I'm sorry but we can't deliver before Wednesday ...", "The figures my team have given me don't explain this quite right but ...", "Sorry but the good colours have gone. We only have blue left."

There is nothing worse than hearing what someone *can't* do.

It was 2pm at the annual planning conference I had just organised for a major manufacturing company. The HR director, Henry Fugelbottom (real person but no, not even close to his real name), took the platform. He leaned into the microphone: "I was hoping to show you the graphs for last month's employee costs ... but there was a glitch on my PC and I couldn't get my PowerPoint to work."

My heart sank as I watched the audience visibly slump down in their seats. No matter what Mr Fugelbottom said from there on, the audience was now standing by for a B-grade speech. And it wasn't just about the graveyard shift timing. We couldn't help ourselves. Henry had delivered a negative in the starting block and it coloured our expectations.

For a few years, I undertook work for one of the big retail building warehouses in Johannesburg. One day, I was invited into a management forum as I had been contracted to handle the opening of their planned new warehouse in Fourways. It was the month of April. Albertus Arterberry, (if you're wondering about the name again ... no, its not), manager of stock control, stood up for his report back. "I'm afraid we didn't manage to keep our stock-levels up at the 95% target we had hoped to reach," he opened nervously, "and we've hit a plumbing problem with the new warehouse complex. So we're not going to open on time."

Well, that was a good pitch. It was all downhill from there for poor old Albertus!

And has anyone out there got a story (or six or seven) related to our service industry? In the middle of writing this very section, my friend Janet spewed venom over the rim of her cappuccino mug one morning. She'd just bought an (very expensive) bed-set from ...

let's call them Beehive Furniture ... and coughed up the requested 50% deposit, agreeing to the other 50% on satisfactory receipt of aforementioned furniture.

On the day of delivery, she was told she had to pay the other 50% before delivery could be executed. "We can't," some lass in the delivery department said in a bored voice, "deliver until you pay. Oh, and I know we said we'd bring it through today but we can't do that. We'll try for next week sometime."

Can't. Can't. Can't. It took two more cathartic frothy coffees and a display of deep breathing that would have earned her VIP status in a childbirth class for Janet to get through that one. There is nothing more off-putting than being told what someone cannot do. An element of human psyche is that we respond well to things of a positive nature and badly to the negative. The rules are simple: If you want to get some bad news across, try doing it in a positive way by explaining

> "If your actions inspire others to dream more, learn more, do more and become more, you are a leader."
>
> John Quincy Adams
> US President
> 1825 - 1829

what you can do. Tell me what you *can* do, not what you can't do.

Beehive Furniture should have enthusiastically promised an early morning delivery on, say, Tuesday the following week. (Later than expected but a positive promise of assured delivery would have been acceptable). As for the additional payment request, you don't threaten a customer with the negative. You get your story and your tone of voice right and only then do you (politely) negotiate any original requests.

Albertus Arterberry would have met with a much better response if we had heard "Despite the recession, we managed to maintain stock levels at 93%. And we're hoping to make that 94% next month." And, as for the planned warehouse opening, the point is he had found the problem and was fixing it. He could have worked a really positive angle for himself. "And the good news is that we've figured out the plumbing problem in our new warehouse and the teams are on it 24 X 7. So we're online for a June launch."

And what of Henry Fugelbottom? He should have squared his shoulders, knowing that none of us would have known he bungled his slide presentation *unless he told us* and said "Anyone besides me tired of looking at PowerPoint graphs? I'll put the stats on the

website this afternoon but for now I am going to focus on the "so what" of those figures. How do employee trends affect our bottom line this year?"

TAKE-OUT: Never underestimate the importance of how you present something - be it in conversation, on a call centre, or on the public platform. Tell me what you can do, not what you can't do.

▶▶ PITHY PLAN

- ▶▶ This is both a matter of attitude and a need for practical planning.
- ▶▶ With regards to attitude, become a "Can-Do" person. Even when facing a problem, focus on the solution and what can be done rather than a wind-up session on the problem itself.
- ▶▶ With regards to practical planning, make sure that you and those around you practise the "yes-we-can" script rather than the "sorry-but-we-can't" script. This relates to how you present a proposal, a report, a speech or even a conversation.
- ▶▶ It particularly relates to a script if you are working with a call centre or any form of frontline communication.

LEADING

Don't mind Prima Donnas ...
As Long As They Can Sing

From a managerial point of view, I suppose Business Utopia would be populated by perfectly behaved, nicely responsive, suitably admiring, deadline focused and definitely obedient employees. Wouldn't that make business life so much easier?

It would also kill any chance of doing something extraordinary.

Every company is divided into different "types". You need them all. Thank your lucky stars for the operational die-hards that produce day in and day out with unquestioning dedication. But you have to make room on your business stage for a few prima donnas. They might be harder to manage and may even be bad team players, but they produce the extra-ordinary - they really can sing!

For almost a decade, I worked in a world populated by Creative Creatures. I co-owned a graphic design company during a heady span in South African business history when design houses were hot and happening. Even in the seriously detailed and production focused world of annual reports and publications (they were all print - as in *paper* - back then), advertising and public relations events, prima donnas were a rare breed of bird you caught, cultivated and, hopefully, kept.

Marlene was a particularly exotic bird who was blessed with an abundance of creative DNA. She was a managerial nightmare. With deadlines looming, Marlene would flick her long hair over one shoulder and lean against the window staring at the clouds, dragging on a continuous chain of cigarettes while consuming cups of her staple diet, black coffee. The rest of the team was head down and shoulder to the wheel for, in that business, a deadline is a DEADline.

In a gale even turkeys can fly

"Now would be good to get those ideas down on paper, Marlene," the team would encourage. "Presentation deadline only hours away ...?" ("Hello? Anybody home?")

"I am trying to connect with the Muses," she would say, inhaling long deep drags of nicotine.

After several hours of "musing", the cigarette smoke around her would be thicker than the volcanic ash cloud that grounded aeroplanes in half of Europe during 2010. But the page in front of her would still be blank.

Muses are useful but not good on deadlines. The only reason she was tolerated by the long-suffering team was because this prima donna could truly hit the high notes. We managed her tightly on output and success ratios rather than more traditional time-in and time-out measures. And the rest of the team learned to work around her erratic and, frankly, selfish approach. But then every graphic studio needed at least one of these exotic breeds in their habitat. You also get the ones that look and act like prima donnas but can't sing. Sometimes this kind of personality is little more than a gigantic cover for incompetence and conceit. A fatal and flawed combination. Such a team-member is a waste of salary and your energy. Furthermore, their presence is likely to drive the good ones away. Everyone has a tolerance line.

TAKE-OUT: Unless you have a fairly unusual business model, don't hunt down every leading lady and matinee idol in town and house them all together behind one curtain. Every good production needs a whole line of supporting cast members and where would Broadway be without the chorus line? It's like a pyramid. You need people to fill roles from the base to the tip. Talented prima donnas have their place at the thin part of the pyramid.

▶▶ **PITHY PLAN**

- ▶▶ It's about knowing what you need and why.
- ▶▶ Analyse your skills requirements very carefully.
- ▶▶ If you need a long dedicated chorus line of operationally minded workers, then don't mess things up by employing hard-to-handle prima donnas.
- ▶▶ If you need a few sparks of Something Extra... then start the auditions.
- ▶▶ Just ensure that you are prepared to manage them appropriately ... and make sure they CAN sing!

LEADING

The *two* e-Mail Rule

Simon sends you a mail. You reply. But Simon has something more to say. So he mails you a reply to your reply. And he copies Phil this time. And you - of course - mail back. Phil has something to say about what Simon says ... so he mails his reply to your reply, which was actually a reply to Simon's mail. So you reply.

We've become a society of keyboard communication.

In the school world, I've conducted complicated conversations via SMS with entire "phone trees" of moms ... without actually speaking to anyone. And it's worse in business. E-mails seem to arrive complete with their own inbuilt artificial intelligence. You are not required to do much except hit "Reply All". And because it's so easy, we do it. Over and over again.

We like the "Two e-Mail" Rule.

If a tricky, ticklish or complicated e-mail conversation goes beyond two bounces of the digital ping-pong ball, then stop typing.

One memorable day in digital business-land, a member of my team reached Breaking Point when an e-mail conversation with a colleague went one click too far. He moved in during a coffee-break and delivered a message of his own. A quick corridor chat would have been so much less painful!

Nothing - repeat nothing - beats face-to-face communication when it comes to sorting out tricky issues in the corporate corridors. It might sound like a small thing but taking control of this kind of communication is a good opportunity to show leadership. Of course there are times when you need the words or agreement in writing but when a brief exchange on e-mail turns into a torpedo path of typed exchanges, copied to all and sundry, you know you've hit Techno Table Tennis syndrome. And no-one wants to be the guy who stops hitting the ball back. I feel the same way about text messages on mobile phones. You send a message to one of your team-members one night asking him to handle a problem the next day. He replies with a question. You reply with the answer. He replies to say, "got it" and "will do". You don't reply "Good for you". Not unless you want a reply like "Thank you" to which you have to reply "You're welcome" to which he replies "Sleep well" and then manners dictate that you reply "thank you, you too".

When it comes to digital communication, don't turn it into normal conversation. If it's a real conversation you're after, then get up out of your chair and go have the conversation. It's still what our species is programmed to do. And it accomplishes the job much more effectively.

TAKE-OUT: If a conversation is starting to turn into Digital Ping Pong, pick up the telephone or, better still, push back your chair and take a walk. This is particularly true when the communication is an argument or point of disagreement. You'll never reach satisfaction when you're arguing with words on a computer screen.

▶▶ PITHY PLAN

- ▶▶ Apply the "Two e-Mail" Rule.
- ▶▶ If you send or have received two e-mails on a subject that is either tricky, filled with discord, not mutually understood and worst of all, a point of complete disagreement that has been copied to all, then:
  - ▶ Pick up the telephone or walk across the corridor.
  - ▶ Now do that old fashioned thing called Talk.

Pithy Pearls

"Our chief want is someone who will inspire us to be what we know we could be."
> Ralph Waldo Emerson
> American philosopher, writer and poet

"Management is efficiency in climbing the ladder of success; leadership determines whether the ladder is leaning against the right wall."
> Stephen R. Covey
> Author: The Seven Habits of Highly Effective People

"I praise loudly. I blame softly."
> Catherine the Great
> Empress of Russia 1762 - 1796

"Wise men talk because they have something to say; fools, because they have to say something."
> Plato
> Classical Greek philosopher, 400's BC

REWARDING

"Flatter me,
and I may not believe you.
Criticise me,
and I may not like you.
Ignore me,
and I may not forgive you.
Encourage me,
and I may not forget you..."

William Arthur Ward
American author and inspirational leader

REWARDING

Contracts (and performance) are *by MUTUAL consent*

So, you're measuring the right things, offering the right reward and still not getting the results? Ah ... but do you have a contract? One of the fundamental principles of communication is to make sure it is properly "two-way". Are you sure the person with whom you are negotiating this measurement and reward agreement - whether for 12 months of performance or specific deliverables on a specific project - has the same understanding of the tasks, the expectations and what the reward will be?

When money and status, or just plain recognition, are at stake, there tends to be a chasm between giving and receiving the terms. There is a solution. Make 'em sign!

A few years back, I did some work for a large weldmesh manufacturing company. They had a fleet of eleven trucks on the road and a somewhat erratic delivery record. Management was facing confusing and contradictory explanations from their trucking managers as to the cause. One minute the maintenance

> You want me to deliver what? By **when...?**

crew got the blame, the next it was the despatch team for issuing unclear delivery details and maps.

So everyone sat around the table to work things out. It took a month. In the end, everyone settled on an agreed baseline. The maintenance team had to have the trucks on the road with a minimum of 96% uptime. No problem, they said. That's our job. The despatch team had to produce a measured 98,1% accuracy of delivery routes. No problem, they said. That's our job. Good. Everyone happy.

Then came the stretch: for every percentage they achieved above the business-as-usual agreement, management would offer reward. Such achievements would require all sorts of effort and commitment so this was no longer about just "doing my job".

They co-created the terms. It involved a fair amount of argy-bargy back and forth across the table but the result was mutually understood performance levels, methods of measurement and rewards.

The final step was the deal clincher. Everyone involved signed contracts. Not an HR employment contract but a renewable yearly "performance" contract that they had created together.

Personally, we apply this approach to every employment situation, project and contract both at work and outside of work. An excellent framework to structure a "performance contract" is the old "Who? What? When?" approach. What must be delivered by whom, how and by when? The tools and methods of measurement should be clear (feedback forms? Tick-lists? Sums on a spreadsheet?) If you do it right, the employee should be able to judge their own success rate even before you book the feedback meeting to discuss their

> "I know you think you know what I said, but I'm not sure you realise that what you heard isn't what I meant."
>
> Warren Keuffel

performance evaluation. Ideally, you should cover both qualitative (behaviour) expectations as well as quantitative (percentages, numbers etc) clauses.

Give some thought to the weighting. Does increasing sales have the same weight as, say, maintaining uptime on the vehicles? What about behaviour? Is innovative thinking a requirement or do you want to place more store on high levels of operational service?

And lastly, be reasonable. We are going to assume you want to keep your team, not drive them away with unreasonable demands. Leave them with room to overperform. Find a way that ensures that result and reward appropriately.

"I know you believe you understand what you think I said. But I am not sure you realise that what you heard is not what I meant."

Originally said on the public platform by either ex-US president Richard Nixon; Robert McCloskey, US State Department spokesman during a Vietnam War press briefing; or even Alan Greenspan, American economist and ex Chairman of the Board of Governors of the US Federal Reserve.

Maybe they all said it? Now *that's* scary.

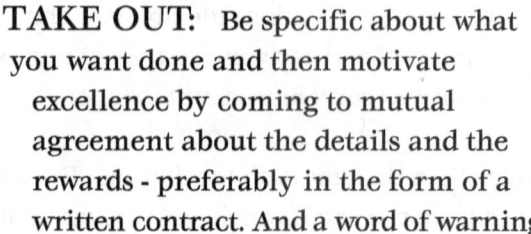

TAKE OUT: Be specific about what you want done and then motivate excellence by coming to mutual agreement about the details and the rewards - preferably in the form of a written contract. And a word of warning - if you don't reward those who go the extra mile, then expect to get exactly what the job specifies - nothing more.

▶▶ PITHY PLAN

- ▶▶ Find yourself a "performance contract" template. Create one from scratch or save yourself a heap of effort and download a basic template off the Internet. Just remember to change it to suit your environment.

- ▶▶ Make sure the form covers the basic areas of activity you need. Think through what you and your company are all about but the categories could include:
    - ▶ Service delivery (external frontline, internal service or both)
    - ▶ Products (development, maintenance or both)
    - ▶ Administration (you could get specific depending on your company)

- Strategy (make sure this dove-tails with the overall company strategy)
- Innovation (ditto above. Innovation can be a large arena!)
- Finance (controlling and managing it or contributing towards its adherence)
- Management

▶▶ Be sure about the macro objectives of your company, division or team. Everyone has to know where you are going and what you want to achieve as a unit.

▶▶ Ask your employees or team members to complete their own performance contract, identifying what they specifically will be undertaking as part of the big plan.

▶▶ Include specifics such as "What" they will be doing, by "When" and "How". They must also identify how they will be measured.

▶▶ Both parties happy with the contents of the performance contract? Good. Now sign.
And halfway through the year, put a feedback session in place. It's kind of silly to wait until the very end of a 12 month period to tell someone off for non-delivery or to adjust the direction of their performance plan.

REWARDING

Measure Right, Reward Right

A key component of a performance contract is the reward bit.

Inside the work environment, one of the safest places to be is within the comfort zone of Activity. Your team members feel fulfilled and genuinely tired out after a long day of working hard and busily. They excelled in producing, sorting, managing and organising. And yet the bottom-line targets, or more to the point, your bottom-line objectives, have escaped delivery. Why? They might have been achieving things but were they the RIGHT things that contribute to your bottom line?

Abraham Maslow and other more latter day psychologists are swift to point out that there is a pecking order when it comes to what motivates people. Most people respond to the basic stuff of life such as money, prizes or a week in Mauritius. Okay, times are tough. Let's make that a weekend in Klerksdorp. Something small that I find works well is a voucher for cappuccino and cake at the local coffee shop. And an extra hour at lunchtime to indulge in it.

Believe it or not, I shot this this photograph through our kitchen window. As the huge project took shape over three months, we just hoped our neighbours knew that we lived 24 km from the sea!

Very few are likely to get giddy over a discreet slap on the back but even a verbalised "thank you" goes a long way to putting a smile on someone's face.

A good manager sees this and knows how to cut to the chase. And a good manager knows what he wants as output. And measures that. It doesn't matter how you get there.

Getting the Measurement and Reward formula right is a crucial part of achieving success. When we launched

Metropolitan into a new financial product area, a core part of the business was a personal loan product. Rewarding the right thing was key. If we over-motivated the call-centre into "selling" loans, we would not only have broken the serious financial laws of "affordability" but also risked the entire business model by piling up a black hole of bad debt. If we over-encouraged the offering of very low-risk loans, we would have landed up ignoring the market segment that needed the money most of all. Again, the business model would have gone for a ball of chalk.

Of course the answer lay, as with anything, in the word "balance". All we're saying is be careful what you choose to reward. You might just get what you asked for.

TAKE-OUT: See through the smoke screen of activity and set clear agreements with your team regarding what they are required to achieve and how they are being measured. People tend only to apply their energy to things on which they are measured. They really stoke up the engines when they are being rewarded for it as well.

A successful manager is one that understands what needs to be done to get the job done, puts the appropriate measurements in place and then rewards performance against those measurements.

▶▶ PITHY PLAN

- ▶▶ Putting it in Place:
  - ▶ Identify the five or so key activities that will be required to achieve the task or job in hand.
  - ▶ Put the measurements in place for those activities. Determine what will constitute the different levels (Acceptable? Achievement? Major success? What about failure?).
  - ▶ Determine the reward for success and the penalties for failure.
  - ▶ Negotiate and mutually agree on the activities, measurement and rewards with everyone involved.
- ▶▶ How to Reward:
  - ▶ Secret rewards for good performance do have their place but for the best results, make this activity very public.
  - ▶ Put in place small along-the-line rewards and moments of recognition to keep interest and motivation alive.
  - ▶ Make a big fuss about the big performers.
  - ▶ Don't ever renege. Psychologically it's incredibly damaging. You'll probably lose your good guys in the process.

REWARDING

Don't Praise a Fish for Swimming

Before we get too carried away with the whole measure, reward and praise thing, we thought we'd apply a timely hand brake. You're working in a business after all. Is it really necessary to give the postman "Performance Award of the Year" for delivering the post? Or the technical team for keeping the computers functioning? Or the drivers for driving?

We have that problem at home. At nine, Ryan is an enthusiastic respondee to tangible motivation. He learned his first spelling by regularly playing the house "Treasure Hunt" that required he follow the trail of paper-based words, each of which had to be sounded out, through every nook and cranny of the house. Of course, there was always a small reward at the end. That's what Treasure Hunts are all about. But he's not four anymore.

"Look! I got excellent marks for my spelling test," he shouted with excitement as he scrambled into the car the other day. "Does that mean I get a treat?"
No, that means he has done what we expect him to do.

So he gets verbal recognition in the proper "well-done" tone of voice and, personally, he gets the satisfaction of knowing he cracked that one. He does have moments where he excels beyond expectations and the ensuing phone call to Butlers Pizza or a visit to the video shop is promptly delivered in recognition of extra performance. However, at Grade 4 levels, we have a long way to go and I don't want him to learn the habit of expecting the world to applaud every time he achieves something. And neither do I need my team to think they get an increase every time they deliver a project on time.

We've already said that a critical element of performance and reward, whether you're talking about staff members or external suppliers, lies in having an understanding or "contract". Doing the job on time, in budget and according to spec is what is expected. Well done. Go home and say, "Yay, I get to keep my job." Don't expect the company to burst into a spontaneous round of applause.

Saved the company 8% beyond budget expectation on the new turbine plant installation? Stretched to 130% of targeted sales? Launched a major new company product that opens up the entire Western Cape market for the first time?

That's when you line up the troops and recognise performance or service, over and beyond the call of duty.

TAKE-OUT: By all means encourage people to perform well and enjoy their job as they strive to achieve. Small forms of recognition and encouragement on a daily basis do wonders for morale. However, showing up for work is not the stuff of public acclamation. Reserve the real admiration, public acclaim and financial reward for those who go beyond their contract and make a real difference.

▶▶ PITHY PLAN

- ▶▶ This all comes down to the details of the performance agreement and contract.
- ▶▶ All levels must agree on what constitutes "doing my job" and what constitutes "going the extra mile".
- ▶▶ Make sure the rewards are known for specific milestones beyond "doing the job".
- ▶▶ Don't ignore those "doing the job". There's always a place for recognition and small rewards to keep morale high.

REWARDING

Don't Just Praise Ideas, Praise Delivery

When it comes to reward and recognition, it's tempting to see only the Creative Composers. The Ideas Innovators. The Virtual Virtuosos. Sure, every company needs them. Without them, you'll find yourself staying firmly on the worn path of doing-things-as-you've-always-done-them. Which, depending on your business model, could be just fine.

But when you put your reward system in place, remember the humble members of the chorus line. No matter how juicy an idea looks on the whiteboard, it's not going to bring about any results without a whole lot of effort. Dreaming up the good ideas is not

where success lies. In the business world, it is delivery that matters.

Haven't you ever noticed how a completely original idea pops into your head ... about a month before you see it in every retailer magazine or on every television show? It's almost like new ideas or trends are carried on air and breathed into brain cells around the world, at exactly the same moment. And if you can get to grips with that, then you'll understand the importance of recognising delivery on great ideas rather than just focusing on invention.

When you recognise a really good original idea, there's always a strong urge to wrap it up and hide it behind a secret password in the "Top Secret" file for fear of attack by those invisible "Idea Hijackers". You might be right about keeping it under wraps for now - but an idea that is never delivered is like a symphony that remains on paper.

If someone brings you a good business idea, reward the inventor but turn the weight of your motivation to urging the delivery team on and forward. It is one thing to come up with a new idea but quite another to actually make it work in the business.

Think of some of the Ideas Inventors of our day. Tim Berners-Lee? Bill Gates? How about Robert Jarvik?

Clockwise from top left: Bill Gates of Microsoft, pictured here during a charitable visit to Southern Africa; Robert Jarvik, Doctor and scientist; Sir Alec Jeffreys, geneticist; Sir Timothy Berners-Lee, computer scientist.

Alec Jeffreys? They would be the first to tell you that without an enormous amount of effort by their respective delivery teams - effort that, one can only hope, that was properly rewarded - the World Wide Web (that would be Tim), the personal computer (Bill, of course), the artificial heart (thank you, Robert) and DNA profiling (that was Alec) would still all be Great Ideas lying in someone's filing cabinet.

TAKE-OUT: The world would be a stagnant and unexciting place indeed without the creative genius of the special few whose calling lies in innovation and invention. However, when it comes to setting the measurement and reward contracts, pay particular attention to the men and women who take someone else's Great Idea and actually deliver it, in good working order, into the commercial world.

▶▶ PITHY PLAN

- ▶▶ Dare we say it - again - it all comes down to what's in the performance contract or agreement.
- ▶▶ Measure and reward the creative sparks who dream up the good ideas but don't measure and reward your Doing Brigade with the same set of rules.
- ▶▶ The Ideas Brigade will have a completely different set of details in their performance contract to the Doing Brigade.

REWARDING

Employees want to have Fun

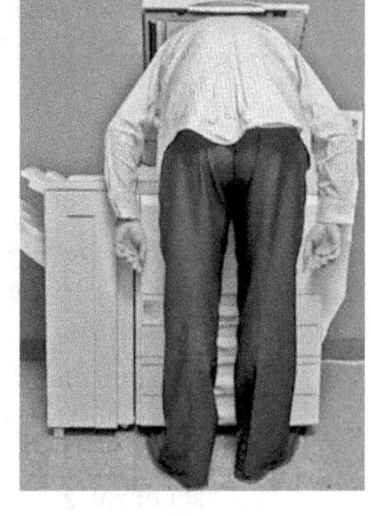

Nothing brings about productivity like sprinkling the corridors with a good dose of fun and giving everyone permission to grin. Life's serious enough without throwing a grey blanket over the work-heap. You know what happens to Jack when he's "all work and no play."

Positive energy breeds positive productivity. You don't have to believe in Chinese Chi (the delicate balance of energy) to see how much more you can accomplish with an upbeat team than one that is moodily stuck to their PC keyboards with a long-suffering air.

During the late 1980's the Johannesburg Stock Exchange had been through a particularly tough

Ending a blue chapter at the JSE with a (fun) dig at management

financial period. A lot of staff members had been retrenched and the air was heavy and blue. Not surprisingly, the employees who made the cut had lost their confidence. They were angry and distrustful.

The organisation had turned the corner and there was a new energetic and positive business strategy in place but how could we lift the negative air and persuade the staff that they were a part of something fresh and good? The answer lay in having some fun. And more specifically, poking a little fun at the object of their anger - management. I suspect some of the great figures that had once graced the trading floor of the JSE would have rolled in their graves if they could have witnessed our "New Strategy" launch, hosted

Above: A bit of fun at the right time goes a long way to creating a motivated team. These were taken at the launch of the new business technology department at Metropolitan at the beginning of Willem's tenure.

as it was on the hallowed floor. Not during trading hours, I hasten to add. One of the activities was to stage a rather unusual fashion show that poked fun at the hated management team. It worked. Somewhere in the middle of all the laughter, the spell was broken. The sense of relief was palpable. We were ready for the next chapter.

In 1998, we launched the new technology division at Metropolitan and, as with any major changes, there was a general air of suspicion. 500 employees crowded into the canteen that had been turned into an impromptu theatre. The theme was Rugby Scrum time and under the temporarily rigged lights and microphones, the "actors" were drawn from the ranks of management and staff. Members of management presented their 12-month plans dressed in Springbok rugby gear. In between the Serious Stuff, we had scrum-downs, whistle parade, film clips and a couple of rugby celebrities to keep things interesting.

The key element here was that the individuals on the new management team were willing to risk things a bit. Making a fool of yourself is a great equaliser. Willem has always believed that it is possible, if not preferable, to be strictly formal about work and yet informal about other things. The challenge lies in drawing and strictly maintaining the line.
Budget and time don't always allow for the Big Event stuff. To introduce some fun and loosen up a little, it's enough to pack everyone off for quick round of putt putt or a furious jostle around a 4X4 training ground. Having fun works like a charm when you most want your team to be serious about their work.

Of course, everything in life is about balance. You'd be hard-pressed to deliver when you're permanently running a Mad Hatter's Tea party.

TAKE-OUT: People deliver best when they are doing something they love, preferably in an environment where they are having fun. Fun is not about being the nice-guy manager. It's about creating an environment where everyone wants to deliver the goods.

▶▶ PITHY PLAN

▶▶ Fun, like every element of business, has to be organised with intelligence, awareness and common sense.

▶▶ It should also be created with a strong expectation of what the outcome will be. English writer, W. Somerset Maugham observed, "Art for art's sake is no better than gin for gin's sake." You could also say that fun for fun's sake (in business) is an opportunity wasted.

▶▶ Create the fun elements of your business plan with purpose. Is it the launch of a product? A new branch? Is it an opportunity to meet clients? Is it to recognise performers and inspire others to do better? Is it a vehicle for delivering important news to everyone? Whatever the "why" of your fun event or activity, let that be the reasoning behind the "what" and the "how".

Pithy Pearls

"We work to become, not to acquire."
Elbert Hubbard
American writer and philosopher

"And as we let our own light shine, we unconsciously give other people permission to do the same."
Nelson Mandela
First "post-apartheid" president of South Africa
1994 - 1999

"Nothing average ever stood as a monument to progress."
A. Lou Vickery
American business writer

"Work and play are the same. When you're following your energy and doing what you want all the time, the distinction between work and play dissolves."
Shakti Gawain
Author

"Anything you're good at contributes to happiness."
Bertrand Russell
English philosopher, logician, mathematician

"It's always worthwhile to make others aware of their worth."
Malcolm Forbes
Businessman, publisher of Forbes magazine

Pithy Pearls

"An acre of performance is worth a whole world of promise."
William Dean Howells, Author

"Ability is what you're capable of doing. Motivation determines what you do. Attitude determines how you do it."
Lou Holtz, American Football Coach

"The greatest thing is, at any moment, to be willing to give up who we are in order to become all that we can become."
Max De Pree

"It's your life, your one and only life – so take excellence very personally."
Scott Johnson

"There are two things people want more than sex and money – recognition and praise."
Mary Kay Ash

"People may take a job for more money but they often leave it for more recognition."
Bob Nelson

SURVIVING

"The reasonable man adapts himself to the world; the unreasonable one persists in trying to adapt the world to himself. Therefore all progress depends on the unreasonable man."

George Bernard Shaw
Irish playwright and author

SURVIVING

Foregone Collusion

Outside corporate corridors' walls, people like surprises. Surprise! You just won a trip for two to Honolulu! *"Great! I'll start packing."* Surprise! I painted the wall and re-carpeted the lounge while you were at your mother's. *"Wow! I just love this shade of pureed pumpkin. What an enterprising and thoughtful husband/wife."* Don't try this at work.

Surprise! I've cracked the formula we've all been working on for months and months and now I know how to restructure the team. *("Who the hell gave him permission to think for me and over my dead body am I listening to his ideas.")*

Surprise! We've launched the new product, done the market-tests, studied the financials and now we're ready to explode onto the scene. *("How come I knew nothing about this? Why are we always the last to know around this joint?")*

The bigger the issue, the more the amount of lobbying that is required. To begin with, have one-on-one chats with the individuals you really need to win over.

Group presentations come later. We suggest conversation, not hard sell. Foregone collusion - and no, it's not a spelling error - means you have to achieve proper mutual understanding, not just a tick-list of people you have dropped in to see.

When you've got something really important to win through, you can't risk grandstanding or presenting at full steam without at least most of your audience already being behind you. Ideally you need to have secured support for your proposal *before* you walk into the presentation room. Another practical reason for applying the rule of Foregone Collusion is to find out who's going to oppose you. Rather know your critics and their criticisms before you take the stand in front of 15 people with your meticulously prepared power point presentation.

We have a brilliant, creative, inventive and enthusiastic friend who is in middle management at one of the big petrol companies. We have yet to see one of his brilliant, creative and inventive ideas actually make it into the real world. Why? Because Alan has an inbuilt mechanism that refuses to engage in foregone collusion. It's not that he's arrogant. It's not even that he's secretive. He's just not figured out the knack of getting his colleagues to buy into his good ideas by playing the right game. He believes his job is to think up the plans and it's up to the rest of management to see the brilliance and make it all real. He works himself to a standstill to make his next presentation even better than the previous one but we know he's going to land up at our kitchen table over another glass of red wine, gloomily reporting back on management's luke-warm response to the morning's pitch.

It's a jungle out there, we urge him. You have to play the game. Peers, superiors, team-members, report-ins all like to feel part of something, no matter who the inventor was. Psychologically, the "not-invented-here" response bubbles up when faced with another fantastic new idea. You have to get the right people on-board before taking the microphone for your big "surprise!" pitch.

Business is a political minefield so don't expect the individuals you approach to share their innermost feelings over a cup of tea but people are generally more forthcoming one on one. At the very least, you will get some sense of the lie of the land.

TAKE-OUT: When you need to sell an idea or reach consensus around a table, make sure you have done your homework, and consensus building, beforehand. This is **not** the time or the place to go for a "sneaky reveal" or the big applause "grandstand announcement." If you want your ideas to see the light of day, make sure you gather supporters along the way, *before* you seek board or committee approval.

▶▶ **PITHY PLAN**

- ▶▶ First identify who you need to influence or at least include.
- ▶▶ Decide how best to accomplish this. A one on one meeting? Sending a copy of a document? A telephone call?
- ▶▶ Now bring them onboard. We're not going for full agreement here. That would be pushing your boat out too far. We're suggesting something more subtle. Engage. Share information. Check their response. Listen to criticism. Acknowledge advice.
- ▶▶ Gather any new information you have now gleaned and use it before going to the next step. At very least, you know who's for and who's against your proposal.

SURVIVING

You've only sold an idea when it becomes
Someone Else's Idea

Let's assume you are not an inventor sitting in a darkened laboratory somewhere with "invention" your sole reason for being. If you are, stop reading. For the rest of you, we assume you are a member of a team in a small or large company. You've got a good idea, right? You've done your homework, written the necessary logical documents and it still makes sense. You've even engaged with all the right parties and made them part of your thinking. Now here's a tough proposal. You might need to make it "Someone Else's Idea" in order to deliver it.

Here's the part where Ego has to be set aside in favour of delivery.

It works in different ways. Let's say your idea is something for your own area or division. You have to deliver and you can't do it alone. So put together a good team with a strong leader. With the right motivation and brief, the team should be able to deliver this next Big Thing. Essential to the formula is making the "delivery team" adopt your idea *as if it was their idea*. Sit in their project planning meetings and offer guidance and direction but note the shift of energy when they take ownership and start running with it. Allow yourself a moment of satisfaction for now the idea has legs.

Now let's say this idea is something for one of the *other* areas in your company (for example, you are in Human Resources or Technology and this is an idea for the sales part of the company). In this case, you need to find yourself a committed and enthusiastic owner. In the process, your idea will loosen itself off you and migrate to the new owner. The concept might even change a little as the new owner adds his own spin. But at least it gets delivered. Have a quick read of the chapter on "Foregone Collusion" before walking away too swiftly. If you follow that advice, you'll still be remembered as the originator of the idea. Your next career move could be dependent on it!

TAKE-OUT: If it truly is delivery you are after, you need to loosen your grip on ownership. If the idea you have remains tucked away in your head or buried on pieces of paper it is not going to do the world, let alone your career, any good. Make sure the people who need-to-know your role in this, know. Then ... let go.

▶▶ PITHY PLAN

▶▶ Identify whether this Great Idea is one within your own area or for another area.

▶▶ Assemble the troops who are best suited for the Delivery Brigade. By this we mean the right department or the right project team. If it's not in your area of influence, this process is a little less direct and requires some "foregone collusion" before it leaves your hands.

▶▶ Once the idea is clearly understood, make sure ownership for delivery lies with the Delivery Brigade. Preferably the one person leading the Delivery Brigade.

▶▶ Now let go. It's no longer yours. It's theirs. It will change and evolve but if you've got the right team on the job, at least it will get delivered.

SURVIVING

Corporate Jujitsu
Better to Deflect than Confront

Business borrows from the martial arts in the case of Corporate Jujitsu. Back in the ancient days of feudal Japan, the sword-toting samurai warriors often had to face situations of confrontation where weapons were either forbidden or the need for stealth rendered them impractical. Their plan B was to use fighting positions such as "pins", "throws", "biting", "kicking" and the painful sounding "joint locks" that deflected and used the attacker's own energy against him, rather than apply head-butting confrontation. The word "jujitsu" translates literally into the "art or science of softness."

In business, applying corporate jujitsu means the same thing - use your opponent's own power to deflect. The key to this tactic is timing and knowledge. On the ancient battlefield, this would have meant getting close to the enemy before making a move. In business, you do the same thing. Take the time to study your opponent - and we could be talking marketplace competitors or just the guy who is after the same job as you - with patience before deciding how to play things. The trick lies in identifying which aspects of his energy you can leverage for your own advantage.

There was a clash of the motor giants a few years back in South Africa when Mercedes Benz launched a television commercial showing just how safe their cars were. Basing their storyline on a true incident, they literally drove a Merc off the precipice of Chapman's Peak, one of the most beautiful but dangerous high cliffs overlooking the Atlantic along the Western Cape coast, to show what a beating the vehicle could take. In the original story, the driver survived the 100m plunge thanks to the fact that he was wearing a seat belt and secondly, of course, because he was driving a Mercedes. Strong stuff.

Enter BMW into the media battlefield. Instead of trying to outgun their competition, they cleverly launched into a swift response with all the agility of jujitsu warriors. They shot a commercial on exactly the same windy road around Chapman's Peak but instead of ploughing the BMW over the edge, they showed the car manoeuvring the extreme corners with "road-stick" appeal. "BMW Beats the Bends", the single

Chapman's Peak, Cape Town, where the Mercedes, BMW and Landrover ads were shot.

line said quietly. Nice. They rode on the energy of their competition to build their own brand.

But wait, there's more. A short time later, a new jujitsu warrior stepped into the already crowded battle ring. Landrover also shot their television commercial along the (now over-used) Chapman's Peak road. But instead of rolling the car down the slopes, the Landie simply drove up the sheer face. Clever stuff. Clever jujitsu.

Of course at the time, the South African advertising authorities had a frothy about "comparative advertising" and it wasn't long before the BMW and Landrover ads were pulled off the air. But here we are, years later, still remembering this great example of corporate jujitsu.

TAKE-OUT: Warfare in the business world isn't always fought in the open. Going up against your enemy, your critics, or even a difficult member of staff, with direct confrontation rarely leads to the right result. Apply stealth and the art of corporate jujitsu and find ways to deflect your opponent's energy and use this to your advantage.

▶▶ PITHY PLAN

- ▶▶ This is a mind game before it becomes a thing of action.
- ▶▶ Consider your "opponent". Consider from all angles, including the ones you know and the ones you don't know. Try this with a healthy dose of objectivity.
- ▶▶ What does your "opponent" do that will provide an opportunity for you to leverage.
- ▶▶ This is the time for clever thinking, not open warfare!

SURVIVING

How Machiavellian!

As the media are only too keen to share with us, there are far too many real-life baddies on this planet. So being the Nice Guy is applaudable. But if you want to get ahead in the business world, you have to temper sugar and spice with a fairly large splash of something else. We're not saying you should draw on the power of all that is evil but we are saying keep your wits about you and don't assume everyone else in the sandpit is going to play fair.

And if you pull something off that brings you the comment: "How Machiavellian of you!" don't hang your head in despair. You haven't turned bad. You've just wised up.

Niccolò Machiavelli was a diplomat in Florence during the 16th century Italian Renaissance. He rose through the ranks of government until the Medici family seized power. He was promptly deposed from office, accused of conspiracy and tortured before being exiled to his estate in Florence. Clearly not the kind of man to go quietly into the still night, Machiavelli

Maybe add in a bit of fear... and respect...

poured all his political knowledge and energy into writing *The Prince,* a now famous study of the exercise of power. It was only formally published after his death.

Since its publication, *The Prince* has enjoyed a somewhat controversial position on the literary Roll of Honour. Whatever Machiavelli's intentions, his legacy is a modern political and business word "Machiavellianism" meaning the "use of cunning and deceitful tactics." History often describes him in less than flattering terms but clearly Florence held him in high esteem. His grave bears the Latin words "Tanto nomini nullum par elogium", which translates as "no eulogy (would be) appropriate to praise such a great name".

We believe you can be a Machiavellian businessman, in the true sense of the word, without laying waste to the corporate ground or killing everyone in your path, an approach the real Machiavelli advocated as necessary - on occasion.

Here's what is good and useful about his writings: Machiavelli's greatest gift was to emphasise the importance of understanding human psychology and how to use it to your best advantage. If you don't "get" how the minds of those around you work, then your chances of making it into a position of power are fairly slim.

Machiavelli advocated that some element of fear was necessary on the path towards leadership ... and, ironically, a step towards being loved by those who follow you. Translated into modern day corporate terms, being everyone's favourite boss 24/7 is not going to win you the kind of respect you need to maintain a position of power and leadership. Sometimes the person at the helm has to put his or her foot down, whether it be a size 12 hobbed boot or an elegant pair of Jimmy Choos with extra spikes.

We're not talking bullying. And we're firm believers in the principle of justice. Fair management is not an option - it's mandatory if you want to retain respect. We picked a couple of his more magnificent and contentious ... but, oh so useful, lessons.

SURVIVING

Machiavellian Prince-iple:
Fake It 'til you Make It

This isn't a verbatim quote from the mouth of the "prince" ... but the sentiment was strongly advocated by Machiavelli. "Pretend you have the power until, eventually, you become the part", he says. Power is not a thing of structure. That is only one element. Think of a powerful person. Nelson Mandela? Barack Obama? Winston Churchill? Jack Welch? How about the CEO of your company? To be a leader you need to be seen as a leader. This means looking like, speaking like, and behaving like the one with the power.

It's interesting how much power is a thing of perception, dependent largely on how that individual comes across. It's all about the strong handshake; the confident speech delivery; the direct eye contact and the way you enter the meeting room. Have you seen Nelson make anything but a grand entrance? Everything about the man oozes Presence.

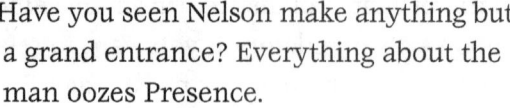

TAKE-OUT: A "prince" is a prince in everything he or she does. It shows in his demeanour, his relationships, his appearance, his choice of friends, his approach to conversations and the way he conducts himself. To many leaders, this is the stuff that comes naturally. Others have to work at it. And if necessary, fake it before you make it. One day you'll wake up and realise this confident leadership role you've been projecting is no longer an act. It's you!

▶▶ PITHY PLAN

- ▶▶ Identify what it is you seek. Recognition of ability or a skill? A reputation for certain behaviour? Admiration for the way you think ... or speak ... or write .... or deliver projects?
- ▶▶ In an ideal world, how would you behave or think or act should you already have those qualities?
- ▶▶ This is not a case of becoming a fake. In the background, learn the skills or practise the behaviour in order to own them yourself.
- ▶▶ In the meantime, consciously project those same elements. Hang out with people who do it well. Watch, learn and then do.
- ▶▶ Eventually your brain and body start embracing these new behaviour and thinking patterns. You become that which you have created.

SURVIVING

Machiavellian Prince-iple
Only the Paranoid Survive

The business world is a funny place when it comes to relationships. We spend so much time at our jobs that eventually the dividing lines between work and friendship become blurred. Some of the best people in my life come from a work environment but, to be blunt, it's rare.

Published 2005 Bedford/St Martin's

Whatever and wherever your place of work, we all spend a lot of hours there and often regard the people with whom we interact as our "friends". Nothing wrong with that as long as you keep a cool, unbiased head when it comes to hiring, firing, mentoring, leading and disciplining. Willem is fond of likening some of his business associates with having a pet snake. You choose to have them in your life.

Published 1998, Univ. of Chicago Press

You enjoy spending time with them and maybe you're even fond of them. But you still have to be cautious when you put your hand in the tank.

TAKE-OUT: Colleagues are not friends. Work with them, co-operate with them, respect them - but do not assume that they will protect you. That is your own responsibility. If you want to keep your job.

▶▶ PITHY PLAN

- ▶▶ Choose your friends, mentors and counsellors with your brain switched on.
- ▶▶ Don't barricade yourself away. We're talking healthy paranoia, not certifiable distrust that lands you locked up in the looney bin for burnt-out stress bunnies.
- ▶▶ Take the counsel of those around you but listen to your own gut and instincts.

SURVIVING

Don't Believe in Your Own
Publicity

Leadership - and management - is not a solo gig. A successful leader needs successful colleagues and report-ins. The nice ones acknowledge this. The ones who run the highest risks are the ones who rely on those around them, ignore their role, and then believe in the myth they have created around their own magical abilities. That is a career looking to fall over.

Apparently Lief Garret, a 70's teen idol, musician and actor, was the first person to utter the words "Don't believe in your own publicity". Yeah, I know. Lief Who? But there are literally queues of celebrities standing in line to help history repeat itself, each of them claiming their spot on the cover of gossip magazines as they crash and burn after mistaking the elixir of super stardom for omnipotence. Depending on your preferred reading, have you seen what has happened to Paris on more than one occasion?
Not the city, the celebrity Hilton heiress. What about Robert Downey Junior? The on-her-game off-her-game Britney Spears? Always fascinating but oh-so-troubled, Lindsay Lohan? And Charlie Sheen?

History is rich with bucket-loads of individuals who have fallen over as a result of too much belief in their own publicity. The movie-making industry and the political arena are particularly fertile ground for this personality flaw. Charlie Sheen (pictured left) picked himself up from a very public professional blow-up and promptly hit the road with a "talking" tour he called Violent Torpedo of Truth. In true Hollywood style, the tour was mainly hated and occasionally loved. During 2011, Julius Malema, (pictured left) erstwhile leader of the ANC Youth League toppled from "Young Lion" of his party to become a man struggling for political and personal survival. Will his flair for managing the publicity machine get him out of trouble this time?

It might be Hollywood that gives us the juicy stories we read in the tabloids but this is by no means the exclusive domain of tinseltown. Woe betide the manager who allows his head-size to become larger than the door-frame. You are only as good as your last success. Don't be lulled into a sense of infallibility by the admiration of the troops. You don't often get straight talking criticism when you are in a position of power. Your team need you to lead them, not use them to polish your own shine.

 **TAKE-OUT:** Don't fall into the trap of self-admiration. Today's achievements very quickly become tomorrow's standards.

▶▶ **PITHY PLAN**

- ▶▶ Stay grounded. No matter how well you are doing on Monday, a failure on Tuesday could mean a fall from grace on Wednesday and you're out the door on Thursday.
- ▶▶ Keep a few very honest advisors or trusted counsellors around that give you a healthy reality check even when you've just received a prize for the business equivalent of walking on water.
- ▶▶ Commit and "attach" to the work and energy of the job.
- ▶▶ Don't attach to the title, the recognition and the corner office that goes with it. It is all fleeting.

SURVIVING

Keeping
Good Company

Never underestimate the importance of the company you keep. This is wisdom for every facet of your life, not just for your business life.

And this particular pithy piece of advice is more hard-core than what it sounds. Having grown up with a father whose mature years have largely been shaped by a deep-rooted love for philosophy, we all regard the ancient Greek philosopher Plato as an honorary family member. He certainly dined with us regularly. Plato I mean. One of the early dinner-conversations in my memory that involved Plato was when I heard that he had written the words, "You are known by the company you keep." And before you dismiss that as hot air from dusty history books, stop and think a moment as to how keeping "good company" can impact on your career.

Success literally rubs off on you. It's not magic. It's one of those irrefutable laws of energy. Something in the line of "like attracts like". And, of course, there is the practical factor that you can learn from someone who has cracked the very formula you seek to master. Not for nothing is mentorship big business these days.

I started out my career with an ad agency called D'Arcy MacManus & Masius. They were mad, bad, brilliant and brash, hectic and frenetic. Sound good? It was, but it didn't fit well with me. I moved into trade publishing, which had plenty of the mad but less of the bad. At the other end of the personality scale, Willem started out with Kloof Gold Mining Company. The brand description or "corporate culture" vocabulary he chooses is "isolated" and "conservative". Neither high-technology nor trend-setting made it to the strategic planning table! He traded it for the perpetual motion of IT and never looked back. Finding a place of employment is more than just grabbing the job.

Going up the ladder of success is not about sitting in the front row of the swamp shouting "Pick me! Pick me!" It requires that you proactively put yourself into positions where the company you keep adds to your project, or job and career. Attend the right conferences. Join the appropriate business associations. Plug into the knowing technology networks. And then apply all this good wisdom in such a fashion that it gets you noticed.

Jenny was a member of the PRISA Public Relations Diploma class I taught for many years.

Keeping "good company" in the modern era! Facebook can be a powerful networking and marketing tool, but one that should be handled with care. Hanging out and exchanging views on this medium of viral communication can be either a positive business experience or bring dire consequences if you sound off about something best kept within boardroom walls.

"I yearn to be a brilliant PR and marketing person," she admitted wistfully during class one evening.

The trouble with Jenny was that she was secretary to an admin manager in a small plumbing company. She didn't attend marketing seminars. She didn't hang out with PR friends. She just sat in her job, waiting for the Angel of Opportunity to come and fetch her.

With some persuasion, she joined a marketing networking group, took on some (unpaid) shadow work for one of the big events organisers in Johannesburg and, within 10 months, landed a job fulltime in their PR team. Coincidental timing? Or keeping the right company?

Keeping a careful selective eye on the company you keep extends into the virtual world as well. "Being connected" has a whole different meaning to what it would have meant a generation ago. It used to be about seeing and being seen. Now it's about finding and being found. Just so long as the virtual company you keep is the right company. Pick and choose your alliances. By all means use any of the social networking platforms to further business. If nothing else, that's where your market is. But if you really feel a need to diss your boss, don't repeat, don't, do it on your Facebook profile. There's nothing private about Internet privacy.

TAKE-OUT: Acquiring an air of power includes hanging out with winners, leaders and people of influence or position. Success begets success. The company you keep - pun intended - has direct impact on your life and job. Choose wisely, using both your heart and your mind.

▶▶ PITHY PLAN

- ▶▶ Figure out your where-I-want-to-be plan.
- ▶▶ What places and which people represent the ultimate achievement of your where-I-want-to-be plan?
- ▶▶ Join the club that deals in this. Sign up for the institution. Read the books. Attend the lectures. Go to the public forums. Click on their websites. Converse on their blogs.
- ▶▶ Spend time with the people who represent what you want to be. Don't walk a mile in their shoes. Just walk alongside them, see the same things, listen to the conversations and breathe in the same air. After all, you're trying to head in the same direction as they are.

SURVIVING

Your Bit of the Planet

While we're on the subject of survival: it is almost impossible in today's world to accomplish success for yourself and your company without embracing a cause of a more global nature.

There are many to choose from. Sadly. Poverty, poor education, AIDS. And then there's that other topical issue about the many ways in which we're killing our planet.

Photo: www.askmen.com

Al Gore, former vice president of the USA, shown here in the movie "An Inconvienient Truth", which met with controversy and accolades alike.

No stirring of any emotion? No bristling of indignation or horror? Then you probably shouldn't worry too much as you are definitely not living on planet earth.

We're not going to drag out our modern day soapbox on the subject - others are doing a far superior job - but the fact of the matter is the big baddies are businesses. And "business" is not a globular mass. It is comprised of individuals.

So even if you do personally consider pollution a (dirty) storm in a teapot, poverty something to shrug apologetic shoulders at, AIDS a disease you can cure with a nice warm shower, education over-rated, green an unfavourable colour, ozone depletion oh-so yesterday, and organic a poor alternative to plastic, then consider this: choosing a social responsibility cause to which you can link your brand is a politically savvy thing to do.

Community issues form part of the fabric of any company and if you want to unite your employees in something that motivates and inspires, strikes a chord with your clients and wins you a whole lot of kudos in the process, then watch the CNN or the SABC news one day and pick a cause.

TAKE-OUT: Whether you embrace community and social responsibility undertakings because it makes business sense or you do it to earn brownie points in the leadership stakes, is less important than the fact that you do something. No generation has faced tipping point dilemmas the way we do this century.

▶▶ PITHY PLAN

- ▶▶ Start with tuning in to the real issues and causes that matter to you and your business. It makes sense to spend your time and energy on something that has clear impact on your business or is a good marriage.

- ▶▶ Watch e-TV News, SABC, CNN and Sky News. Listen to the radio. What are the issues grabbing headlines? Get up close and knowledgeable with what's rumbling right now.

- ▶▶ Once you've selected your cause, go into business mode. Create a business plan outlining how you are going to contribute. Use the "why" "what" "where" "when" and "how" formula to make it a business plan rather than a well-meaning but emotional decision.

- ▶▶ Align brand, public relations, marketing and human resource activities with the business plan. Social responsibility is a two-way street. Your cause must win but so can you.

Pithy Pearls

"Let everything you do be done as if it makes a difference."
William James
American psychologist and philosopher

"There is nothing like returning to a place that remains unchanged to find the ways in which you yourself have altered."
Nelson Mandela
Ex president of South Africa, Nobel Peace Prize winner

"Success is simply a matter of luck. Ask any failure."
Earl Wilson
American newspaper columnist

"A man cannot be too careful in the choice of his enemies."
Oscar Wilde
Irish poet, playwright and novelist

"What one sees depends upon where one sits."
James R. Schlesinger
Previously US Secretary of Defence

"We are what we pretend to be, so we must be careful what we pretend to be."
Kurt Vonnegut Jr

Pithy Pop-Biz

On our way out, we thought we'd toss a few more quick pithy phrases at you. Some of them are so familiar you've probably heard them many times before without stopping to consider what they actually mean. Most of them are what we call "suitcases" in that they look nice and neat and small at first glance, but if you open them up and dig around, you'll find they are all pretty big concepts that should make you think really hard!

Today's Achievements are Tomorrow's Standards

If you think everything is going well, you're not in full possession of all the facts

Technology is like a bus. Only get on it after it is going your way

Today is the Tomorrow you Worried about Yesterday

The only Constant is Change

Cash Cows Need to be Fed

WILLEM: The CV Stuff

Essentially left-brain, Willem has applied his non-negotiable sense of order to many major corporations throughout the past 35 years. He qualified with an honours degree in electrical engineering but, after being put to work changing light-bulbs at one of the big mining companies (true story), decided that a different type of company with a different career path beckoned.

Post-graduate qualifications in management and IT led to several senior posts in Information Technology. He can still out-jargon most young PC techies and knows how to open up and rearrange the innards of a PC with the precision of a soldier dismantling his gun. By the turn of the century (21st not 20th) he had been lured deeper into strategic thinking. A stickler for detail, his true calling lies in applying all the sciences to business bottom line.

Strategic planning and new venture implementation, a career he pursued for over a decade, has been a perfect match for his big picture mentality.

Over the years, he held senior management positions with Barlow Data and the South African Bibliographic Network (SABINET), was Chief Information Officer for the Johannesburg Stock Exchange and later for Anglo American Corporation. Then, after nine years as Chief Information Officer for Metropolitan, he became group executive head of Strategic Ventures and a member of the Metropolitan Life board.

Nowadays he continues to apply his knowledge and experience within the financial services industry to new ventures of his own, and occasionally co-writes my books to make them more "pithy".

WENDY: The CV Stuff

For the first couple of decades, I got to grips with a different sort of technology to Willem's IT world. Mine was a world of advertising, electronic media, public relations and multi-media events in a time before PC technology made it a converged science. I still remember when multi-media shows involved 35mm slides that had to be counted and synchronised by hand.

A devotee of ink on paper, I spent a good few delicious years managing editorial teams for trade publications, corporate annual reports and brochures, magazines, brand management publications as well as a range of trade business books. Feeling like a camp-traitor, I crossed over from paper and print publishing to things-digital in the late nineties. Even I had to admit that the arrival of the Super Information Highway aka (later) the Internet, was about to change the face of - well - everything.

For many years, I ran my own corporate communications company. My clients were mainly from the world of Information Technology and finance. It was a life chapter of event organisation, press and media handling, public relations, strategic communications work and motivational leadership training. I firmly retained my "visitor" status around the formal corporate business world until the opportunity of leading the team that was to launch Metropolitan into the web world proved irresistible. Then, early in the century (I thought we agreed - 21st not 20th) I joined the strategic innovation team for Metropolitan where I remained, happily working back-to-the-future, for almost a decade.

Nowadays, I apply my (mainly right brain) thinking to shared business ventures with Willem. I haven't stopped my love affair with the ink and paper reality of freshly printed books. I just channel that love for the written word into writing books that I occasionally allow Willem to co-write. But only when I need to trim them into something a little more "pithy".

A Word or 2 of Thanks

Acknowledgements and recognition of photographic sources:

Our thanks to the Johannesburg Stock Exchange, Anglo-American Corporation, Chartis (the-company-formerly-known-as-AIG!), Metropolitan Life and Sabinet for allowing us to share some of the stories gleaned from our mutual memory banks.

And to the individuals who were brave enough to let us name names in our attempt to glean pithy wisdom - Jan Cronje, Pieter Henning, Claire Rosekilly, Colin Wright, Christo Diederichs, Nigel Adams and Janet Bell - thank you. Thanks, Mom, for the insight into how your world of art is not that different to the world of business. And Dad - where would we be without Plato? Philosophy truly is an approach to life, not a thing of dark shelves and dusty libraries.

Claire, thank you for lending us your usual flair and professionalism in the design and layout of this book. Meryl Zeidler - thank heavens for at least one teacher friend who still practises the art of meticulous proofreading and refuses to compromise when it comes to proper English "as She is Written"!

To the colleagues, friends, business associates and even the unexpected strangers who read our early manuscript and offered sage advice, we thank you. But especially, we are grateful to Arthur Bell for his enthusiastic and detailed contribution to finding just the right stories and quotes and to Mark Wilkes who was brilliant in spotting the important obvious and made a gift of it to us.

To the companies that no longer exist but which, nonetheless, were part of our personal journeys and the business wisdom remembered here - thank you, anyway. You may be long gone but the lessons we shared with you remain.

Wendy & Willem

The problem with business wisdom is that the good ones have many fathers while others remain mysteriously as orphans. We've done our level best here to give true and proper acknowledgement to our sources, partly because we need to in order to tread on the right side of publishing law, but also because we regard this book as a tiny springboard that will hopefully take you to some great reading material and sources of far wiser people than ourselves. Our thanks to the great minds we have drawn on during our years in the business world ... and within the pages of this book.

Bibliography

Strategic Planning Not Fast Forwarding the Past
"The Age of Intelligent Machines" by Ray Kurzweil (MIT Press 1992)
"The Age of Spiritual Machines" by Ray Kurzweil (Penguin 2000)

Don't Boil the Ocean
"In Search of Schrodinger's Cat: Quantum Physics and Reality" by John Gribbin (Bantam Books 1988)
"The McKinsey Way" and "The McKinsey Mind" by Ethan M. Rasiel (McGraw-Hill)

Hands-On Ansoff
"Strategies for Diversification" by Igor H. Ansoff (Harvard Business Review Vol 35 Issue 5 Sept-Oct 1957)
"Business the Richard Branson Way" (Capstone 2002)

Palimpsest
www.facebook.com
www.sixdegrees.com
www.friendster.com
www.linkedin.com
www.myspace.com
www.sairr.org.za

Know What You Don't Know
"Six Thinking Hats" by Edward de Bono (Little Brown and Company 1985)

Brake Into the Corner
www.philosophyschool.com

Don't Take the Monkey On Your Back
"Management Time: Who's Got the Monkey" by William Oncken and Donald L. Wass (Harvard Business Review 1974)

How Machiavellian!
"The Prince" Niccolo Machiavelli (Bantam Classics 1984)

"Be sincere;
be brief;
be seated."

Franklin D. Roosevelt
President of United States of America 1933 -1945

www.ingramcontent.com/pod-product-compliance
Lightning Source LLC
Chambersburg PA
CBHW061507180526
45171CB00001B/68